HIMALAYAN STYLE

HIMALAYAN STYLE

THOMAS L. KELLY

CLAIRE BURKERT

Lustre Press
Roli Books

TEXT © Claire Burkert, 2014

FOREWORD © Robert A.F. Thurman, 2014

PHOTOGRAPHY © Thomas L. Kelly, 2014, except for the following:

Chris Buckley	p. 147-i, iii
Claire Burkert	pp. 31-ii, 57-iii, 58-i, 60-ii, 68, 97-i, ii, 115-i, 128-i, 129-i, 145, 165, 180-i, 183-ii, 232, 233, 245-i
Nicholas Dawson	p. 222-i
Phillipe Garcia	p. 122-ii
Charles Gay	pp. 148, 149
IQ Lab, Bangkok	p. 131
Stanislaw Klimek	pp. 66, 67, 69
Tim Linkins	pp. 198, 200-ii, iv, 201, 202-i, ii, 203, 236-i, ii, 237
Stephanie Odegard	pp. 147-ii, 197-ii, iii, 214
Thomas Schrom	pp. 74, 75-i, 77-ii, 81, 128-i, 130
Shakti Himalaya	pp. 190-i, iii, v, vi, vii
Clive Sheridan	p. 129-ii
Studio Mumbai	pp. 190-ii, iv, 191-i, 192, 193

DESIGN: Thomas Schrom

DESIGN SUPPORT: John Hubbard and Claire Burkert

MAP: John Harrison

ISBN: 978-81-7436-888-1

First published worldwide in 2014
by Roli Books
M–75, Greater Kailash-II Market
New Delhi-110 048, India
www.rolibooks.com

Printed and bound in China

PREVIOUS PAGE:

Krishna plays his flute in a shrine in Patan, Nepal.

RIGHT:

The painted room used by the priest of Kuthu Math, Bhaktapur, Nepal, for rituals and prayers.

CONTENTS

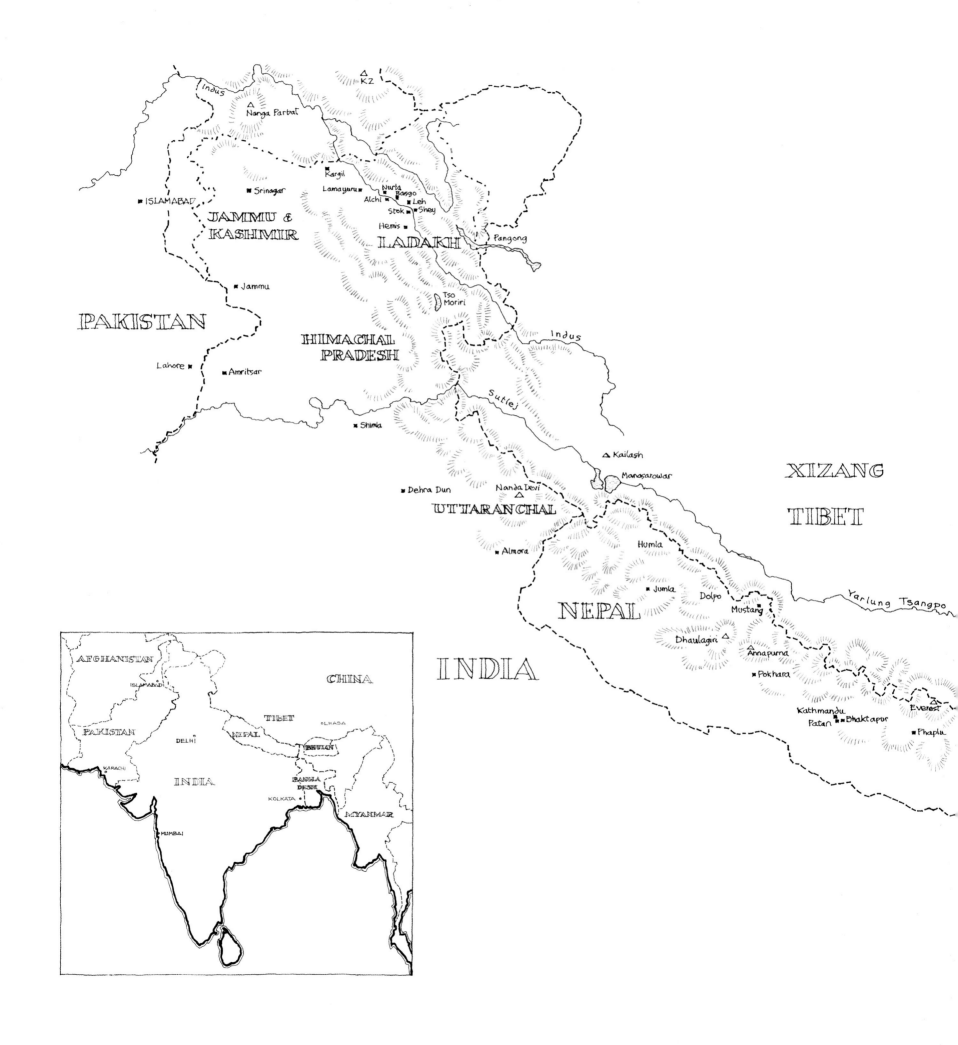

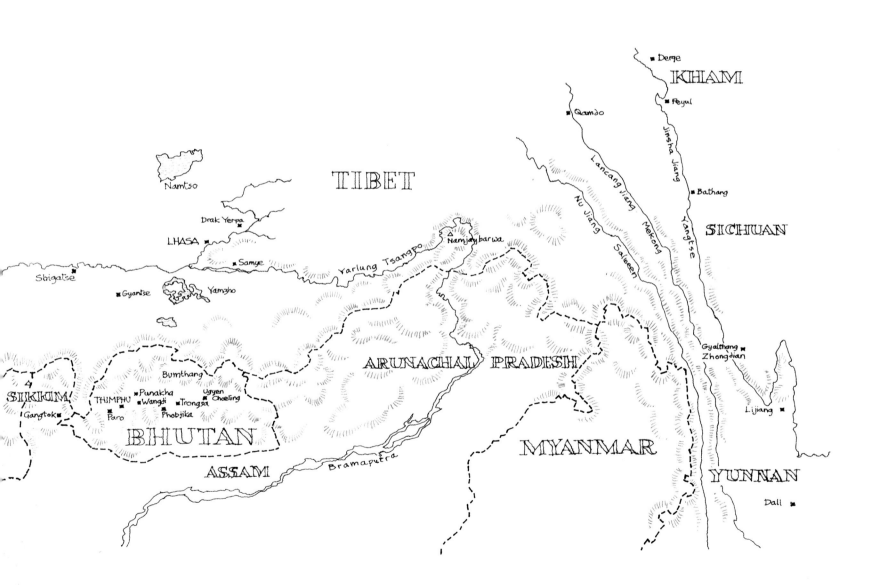

Derge

KHAM

Feyul

Qamdo

TIBET

Namtso

Drak Yerpa

LHASA

Samye

Sbigatse

Gyantse

Yamzho

Yarlung Tsangpo

Namjaybarwa

Bathang

SICHUAN

Jinsha Jiang

Lancang Jiang

Nu Jiang

Mekong

Salween

Yangtse

ARUNACHAL PRADESH

Bumthang

SIKKIM

THIMPHU

Punakha

Wangdi

Ugyen
Choeling

Trongsa

Gangtok

Paro

Phobjika

BHUTAN

ASSAM

Bramaputra

MYANMAR

Gyalthang
Zhongdian

Lijiang

YUNNAN

Dali

FOREWORD

This is a beautiful, utterly luscious book, and I am pleased to welcome it in this foreword!

'Himalayan Style!' What is it? Why is it so beautiful, at least to my eye, and obviously to Thomas and Claire?

The Himalayas were the axis mundi of the Indic peoples, the high sources of their holy Ganga and most of their life-sustaining rivers. Himalayan Buddhists believe that the jewel qualities of the 'Himalayan Style' begin with the inconceivable presence of Shakyamuni Buddha himself. The Buddha consciously chose to reincarnate in a kingdom in the fertile plain below the massive Himalayan wall. He first descended from the Akanishtha heaven to a heaven nearer the earth, the Tushita Heaven of Satisfaction. While giving teachings to the gods and bodhisattvas there, he scanned the planet below until he found his perfect parents.

Each subsequent moment of the Buddha's presence, from his gestation to his full enlightenment, resonated around the planet in just such an inspiring way.

After the Buddha had demonstrated his newfound way to live and die in love with all of life, the Indic culture developed into a civilization based on realistic insight into the nature of mind and body, thus enabling an ever more refined enjoyment of the generous reality revealed. From it came extraordinary traditions of art and science, predating Architectural Digest, and the whole modern 'Art of Living' literature by millennia!

In the context of this beautiful book, this civilization expressed itself in designs that reflect the sensitive architecture of the enlightened, the visualized architecture of celestial buddhas and bodhisattvas. The mandala principle became the paradigm for landscapes, mansions, rooms, furniture, dress, and style of joyful living.

It was not until we spent a year in 1970-71 in Almora in the Kumaon, a part of India very near the Nepal border, on the old pilgrimage route to Mount Kailash, that I began to have a sense of this 'Himalayan Style'. We were living with my family in a cottage on a ridge near the Kasar Devi temple, looking north and east at the highest mountains in India, Nanda Devi and Trishul, both at over 26,000 feet. Below the ridge, the valley dropped away thousands of feet, with every inch beautifully terraced by the loving hand-labour of hundreds of generations. To the south were views of the vast fertile plains of India, watered by the mineral-rich waters from the Himalayas. Living there, we had a timeless feeling that we were on the slopes of the axis mundi, the centre of the world, near the link between heaven and earth. We could feel the divine graciousness of Lord Shiva and Lady Uma, both in their Hindu and their Tantric Buddhist forms, radiating their loving energy from their Mount Kailash home just out of sight beyond the great wall of snow peaks that loomed above.

We were living in a simple cottage on the Snow-view estate, much more humble than the lovely mansions and gardens of Kathmandu, the elegant monasteries of Ladakh, Bhutan, and those surviving in Tibet. Yet in its simple way, it resonated with the heavenly elegance and beauty radiating from the divine and buddhine mandalas above. These Himalayan archetypes luminously touch and shape everything beneath them – landscape, buildings, the people's styles of dress, their gestures, and especially their speech, colloquial and very different but all deriving from the Sanskrit mantric language of the gods.

So then, enjoy the beauty of this book, a precious window onto the 'jewel qualities' of the world floating in the gracious aura of the Himalayas! We can be grateful to Thomas and Claire for opening it up for us, and congratulate them for their creative effort!

Robert A.F. Thurman

A field of whitewashed chortens
below Shey Palace, Ladakh.

INTRODUCTION

Thomas Kelly came to Nepal in 1980, I in 1985, and what followed were rich years working and travelling throughout the Himalayan region. While taking part in the life inside temples, homes, lodges and other Himalayan buildings, we were introduced to a wide range of architectural and interior styles. Our shared love of vernacular design inspired us to make a book that examines a number of Himalayan styles, from ancient to contemporary, rural to urban, and sacred to secular. Many images in the book come from mountainous areas where Tibetan culture and religion are dominant. We also present styles of life in the Himalayan foothills and the Kathmandu Valley. A particular focus is Kathmandu as we know it well, and it is here that a dynamic interchange between indigenous and foreign cultures has resulted in new interpretations of traditional design.

In the time that we have lived in Asia, Thomas and I have seen remarkable changes in rural areas and in Himalayan cities such as Kathmandu, Thimpu, and Lhasa. There is no Shangri-la whose beauty is resistant to outside pressures and change. Himalayan styles are not static – nor would we wish them to be. As is apparent on these pages, Himalayan style is ever-evolving, absorbing the ideas of cultures within and outside the region. At the same time, we have chosen a number of buildings to document because they exemplify what we characterize as 'shelters' or 'sanctuaries' of historic and lasting beauty. Himalayan shelters can be monumental buildings or small domestic structures that protect people who live in demanding and often harsh environments. The monasteries of Tibet have long served as sanctuaries for spiritual contemplation and study. Today the words 'shelter' and 'sanctuary' can also be applied to museums that preserve art and precious objects, or to a public garden that offers a peaceful atmosphere to local residents and travellers.

The Tibetan-style lock of the main shrine of Uku Bahal, Patan, Nepal. The phenomenal artistry of the Valley's Newar artisans is manifest in the grill's lotus and *dorje* motifs created by repoussé and the small lost wax cast statues attached. Lock rings are shaped like hands. Two images of snake virgins with intertwining snake bodies hold their hands in a devotional pose.

The 13th-century Alchi Monastery complex, Ladakh.
Simple white exterior walls of stone and mud mortar
contrast with red painted parapets.

RIGHT: The Tabo Monastery compound in Spiti Valley, Himachal Pradesh is
comprised of nine mud-plastered temples and twenty-three chortens. Founded
in 996 AD, the monastery is now a World Heritage Site.

Given the tremendous breadth and history of art and architecture in
the Himalayan region, it is not easy to limit our focus to elements of
'style'. The styles (colours, materials and forms) of religious buildings or
village homes are inseparable from culture, environment and religion.
But what we can identify, very simply, is a staircase or a window that is
an example of beautiful design that can inspire fresh forms. In the
beginning chapters we have selected elements of style in historic sites
that capture and delight the eye. Then in contemporary museums, homes
and gardens we find re-use and re-interpretation of traditional design
vocabulary. This is a book with a mission. We hope that *Himalayan Style*
will spur interest within the region and around the world in the unique
aesthetics and skills that we value highly.

Our selection of places is personal, based on our travels and the
people we know. We do not claim to have covered all the styles in the
Himalayas, and no doubt we will forever be seeking to document new
buildings and crafts that are unique to this region. What we choose to

focus on within a building also relates to our personal tastes and
interests. For instance, the bright wall colours of monasteries, some with
a shiny patina, resonate with me; and I wonder how I might repeat the
same combination of bright colours somewhere else – in a room of our
Kathmandu house, or on a carved frame made by the Tibetan craftsmen
with whom I work in Gyalthang.

The first section of this book focuses on historic monumental
structures: monasteries, dzongs, temples, palaces, and houses of nobility.
We praise efforts to preserve traditional architecture and to find new
purposes for historic buildings. Models of adaptive re-use of historic
structures are the Patan Museum, a restored and adapted royal palace in
Nepal, and the Tower of Trongsa Museum, a transformed watchtower of
Bhutan's Trongsa Dzong. In Ladakh, the 17th-century house of a royal
secretary was rescued from ruin and converted into the Ladakh Arts and
Media organization (LAMO). Other notable efforts in Ladakh, such as
the restoration of three Maitreya temples in Basgo, preserve important

religious structures so that they can continue to be used by local people. We also present a fresh initiative by the Drukpa Trust under His Holiness the Dalai Lama's patronage to create a school where education reinforces the value of Ladakhi culture.

Sacred rituals and festivals colour our experience living in the Himalayas. Making offerings to the gods is an essential activity of each day. Chortens (*chaityas*), prayer walls, prayer flags and *mani* stones, manifesting powerful spiritual belief, have joined the landscape of Himalayan mountains and valleys. In the second section, entitled 'Design and Devotion', we embrace the acts of devotion that are inseparable from daily life, including the rituals that determine the design and process of building a home.

'Traditional Living in the Himalayas' pays tribute to the wealth of vernacular architecture in rural settlements. It is here that Himalayan style has immense variety and innovation. We cannot know who designed the first Tamang or Humli house, or who first chose the scheme of stripes for a Dolpo blanket or the shape for a wooden butter churn. But traditional local design, so closely tied to the local environment, is timeless. Historic estates in Bhutan are interesting examples of indigenous noble style. Finding a new purpose in the 21st century, some of the estates have now been turned into hotels or museums. Similarly in Ladakh, the ancient homes of ministers await restoration by their descendants, who hope to turn them into travellers' homestays.

Many interiors of Himalayan buildings are humble, with little furniture or decoration. In Sherpa and Ladakhi communities an abundance of cooking vessels attractively displayed on kitchen shelves indicates the prosperity of the household. Houses in Ladakh often have two kitchens, one for summer and one for winter, each with an

attractive ceramic or decorated steel stove: in winter the whole family will sleep on carpets around the hearth. Over time, Tibetan peoples have developed a wide variety of interior decorative furnishings, which often originated in the monastery and later were adapted for private residences. The early Tibetan carpet weavers and furniture makers would have been surprised that Tibetan furnishings and carpets would one day be so highly valued and used in homes throughout the world.

After surveying architecture and interiors developed in monasteries, temples, estates and village dwellings, we arrive at 'Himalayan Retreats and Trails'. Many unique accommodations have been created in mountainous regions for tourists. Hotels and restaurants in the Tibetan town of Gyalthang combine local design with Western elements that increase comfort in a high-altitude environment. Such tourist destinations also offer access to authentic local culture – as exemplified by the Hotel del Sherpa in Solu Khumbu, Nepal, with its dining room painted richly in the local Buddhist tradition. From the hotel you can make a day trip to Chiwong Monastery, and in the autumn you can witness the *cham* dances performed for the Mani Rimdu festival.

Some recently built retreats mark new directions for Himalayan architecture. The clean, simple design of 360 Leti, a mountain resort in India's Kumaon region, has incorporated the materials and methods and skills of local craftspeople. Bhutan's minimalist Amankora lodges do not merely nod at tradition – they are fully inspired by it. The Amankora Paro mirrors the rammed earth ruin of Drugyal Dzong nearby, whereas the Amankora Bumthang appears to respond to its detailed neighbour, the Wangdichholing Palace, with contrasting minimalism.

The Kathmandu Valley, unique in its mix of peoples and cultures, is the focus of our last chapter. The tremendous Newar artistic heritage in the Kathmandu Valley has drawn the interest of artists, designers, and architects from around the world. Here we can only name a few of the gifted artisans who are so essential for preserving and continuing the skills of stone and wood carving, lost-wax casting, repoussé, thangka painting and other Newar arts and crafts.

Also vital to the Valley's heritage are designers and craftspeople who are finding new applications for traditional skills and adding twists to Himalayan designs. Kathmandu's Pipalbot, a lifestyle store and meeting place brings together many craftspeople from Kathmandu and demonstrates how traditional crafts integrate with modern decor. Stephanie Odegard is one among a number of foreign and local designers who have reinvigorated Tibetan carpet making, creating rich 'paintings' of Himalayan patterns and colours. Pasang Tsering's new textiles that utilize pieces of traditional Tibetan aprons are an example of how Himalayan style is dynamic: here a textile tradition continues to evolve and adapt without losing any of its Tibetan character.

View to a stupa through a gateway made of dry-stacked stones in Solu, Nepal.

ABOVE:

The paved courtyard and gallery of Gompa Soma, Leh, Ladakh, built in 1840 and restored by the Tibet Heritage Fund.

RIGHT:

A lit niche in the home of architect Rohit Ranjitkar, Patan, Nepal.

We conclude *Himalayan Style* by looking at some of the private homes and havens in contemporary Kathmandu, and showing how traditional and new Himalayan furnishings and textiles are used today. By beginning with an examination of ancient Himalayan architecture and important restoration projects, and ending with examples of contemporary urban living, we wish to demonstrate the tremendous vitality, range, and potential of Himalayan forms and designs. We emphasize the urgent need to keep alive for the future traditional art, architecture, and building practices. At the same time, we encourage the necessary development of new Himalayan design. We extend our appreciation to the people of many different communities and professions – monks, farmers, artists, architects, carpenters, and many more – who are contributing to the conservation and perpetuation of unique Himalayan styles.

PART 1

THE VITALITY OF TRADITION

Preservation efforts across the Himalayan region have kept historic architecture alive for traditional uses as well as exciting new purposes. Of great monasteries and temples in Tibet, many magnificent structures are tragically lost forever. But in communities throughout the region, from Ladakh to Eastern Tibet, temples and monasteries are undergoing repair and rejuvenation by skilled builders, artists, and craftsmen. Controversial as the process of renewal can sometimes be (as what is new cannot simply replace the old) the style that is so unique in Tibetan monasteries lives on in the use of colour, materials, and organization of space. Moreover, artisans are creating new treasures such as the magnificent Maitreya statues that have been erected in ancient temples in Ladakh.

Bhutan is tending to its impressive *dzongs*, with the Tower of Trongsa Museum, a dzong watchtower transformed into a museum, providing an example of how innovation can bring new life to a structure that has outlasted its original purpose. In Nepal, the royal squares of cities in the Kathmandu Valley are active with events that range from ancient religious festivals to contemporary art installations. In the following chapters we view elements of traditional style of important Himalayan structures and see how these structures are being rejuvenated in the 21st century.

The fortress wall at Shey, Ladakh, dates to the 15th century. Beyond it lies the recently restored 17th-century Shey Palace complex that includes an imposing stupa with gilded spire.

Tibetan Monasteries and Temples

We contemplate Tibetan religious style starting with the Lhasa Jokhang Temple, around which you do *kora* (circumambulation) at dawn or in the late sun of the day. This temple, which stands at the heart of the Tibetan Buddhist world, has at its core the cosmic representation of a mandala. Nepalese artisans who, under King Songtsen Gampo, first constructed the temple in the 7th century closely followed the floor plans of early Indian monasteries (*vihara*). The vihara's mandala layout included a central assembly hall and inner sanctum with a pathway encircling the hall providing access to important shrines. Over the centuries came further developments in design and construction, some indigenous, some from China or elsewhere in Asia. The Jokhang became a classic Tibetan monastic complex, and so grew other monasteries, temples, and nunneries all across the Tibetan world, emerging magnificently monumental and shaped by shifts of power and the spread of Buddhism. The religious architecture that today we view as 'Tibetan' combines the influences of many cultures that crossed the Himalayas and met in Tibet.

The Potala Palace was also built by Songtsen Gampo in the 7th century and was greatly expanded during renovation under the 5th Dalai Lama ten centuries later. Bordered by impressive zig-zagging staircases, the fortress-like exterior of the Potala evokes the dual forces of political power and religion. Such buildings are remarkable to behold, particularly against the deep blue sky of a Tibetan day. Built of stone and mud brick, the outer walls of many buildings of a monastic complex gleam with whitewash: white represents the Buddha and also good fortune. Buildings that are painted dark red (such as the Potala's 'Red Palace') are places with sacred power. Red is also the colour of inner sanctums and protector chapels.

You will notice the exterior walls' artful placement of stones and then the *penbey* frieze, a horizontal band below the roof that is made of brushwood (shrubby cinquefoil or tamarisk) whose ends face outward. The frieze is painted brown or dark red, in striking contrast to the white masonry walls. It is a fascinating detail of Tibetan religious buildings, adding a sense of gravity to the overall composition and so distinct in its earthy texture. The frieze may be punctuated by plaques with auspicious symbols or *melong* – gilded copper or white painted disks suggesting mirrors. On the roof, asserting the building's sacred power, are gilded copper victory banners that symbolize the triumph of Buddha's dharma.

The impressive stepped entrance to the
Potala Palace, Lhasa, Tibet.

TIBETAN MONASTERIES AND TEMPLES: ELEMENTS OF TRADITIONAL STYLE

ABOVE: The gilded canopy roofs of the Potala Palace are topped with spires (*ganjira*) symbolizing connection to the cosmos. The auspicious knot (*pata*) symbol is appliquéd onto yak-hair curtains.

LEFT: Samye Monastery seen through prayer flags.

OPPOSITE CLOCKWISE:

The magnificent Potala Palace seen from the Jokhang Temple roof with two deer and the wheel of dharma in the foreground.

The mythical water creature called a *makara* adorns a corner of the Jokhang roof.

Gilded copper victory banners called *gyeltsen* on the roof of the Jokhang.

Walls and ceilings of the Potala's interior are brightly painted.

A colourful woolen curtain hangs in a doorway of the Potala. Wooden stair railings are finished with decorative brass casings.

STONE, METALWORK AND THE PENBEY FRIEZE

LEFT: At Samye Monastery, the main building (*utse*) has inward sloping whitewashed stone walls and represents Mount Meru. The middle-floor balcony is enhanced by a row of small stupas and the horizontal red-painted bands indicate that the building is religious.

TOP: Exquisite traditional masonry employs layers of hammer-dressed rocks with smaller stones in-between.

ABOVE: Gilded copper metalwork on the Jokhang.

RIGHT: Similar to the rock wall above, irregularly shaped stones are placed in rows with smaller stones filling the gaps. The maroon-coloured frieze made of shrubby cinquefoil or tamarisk is called penbey. White circles painted above the frieze are a typical detail resembling beam ends.

VIBRANT INTERIORS

Within the monastic compound use of colour may be unrestrained. The bright primary and secondary colours used in Tibet have significance: blue symbolizes air, red is fire, green is water, and yellow the earth. White represents air and wind. Walls inside the Potala and the Jokhang Temple are painted in exuberant orange, yellow or green and bordered with stripes of symbolic Tibetan colours.

A short green and red curtain is often painted just below the ceiling. Ceilings may have secondary beams painted bright blue with infill timbers painted in contrasting colours. Brackets and primary beams are intensely decorated with flowers, dragons, and other auspicious images.

CONTINUITY AND CHANGE: PODORONG MONASTERY, NEPAL

In recent years, new Tibetan Buddhist monasteries have been established that exhibit variations in traditional design. Here young monks are housed in a white cement residence that is still colourful with door curtains and hanging robes. Following tradition, however, the temple building exhibits richly-painted murals while a large paved courtyard allows space for religious ritual.

ABOVE: Young monks in residence at Podorong Monastery, Bouddha, Nepal.

RIGHT: Monks' robes hanging on a rail and traditional boots are depicted in a mural at Podorong.

LEFT: Monks entering the courtyard, which is painted with auspicious symbols for the Tibetan New Year.

The portico of Drepung Monastery is supported by giant columns and richly decorated with murals.

Golden dragons, each clutching an auspicious conch shell, and a pattern of mountains and clouds are painted on the temple door of the Talok Monastery in northern Kham.

THE SACRED ENTRY

The entryway of a temple conveys its importance: from here you proceed into a sacred space. In contrast to the building's unadorned exterior masonry walls and its windows bordered in somber black, walls of the portico bear colourful murals rich with Buddhist iconography. Gripped between the claws of Yama, the god of death, the wheel of life is often depicted here, showing disturbing pictures of suffering that urge one on to the path to enlightenment. Images of the Guardian Kings in their opulent robes and fancy boots are painted on either side of the door to offer protection to the temple.

Further emphasizing the significance of the doorway are several sets of carved jambs, one enhanced by *pema-chudzo*, a design of stacked cubes, which translates as the 'stacking of religious law'. Door pulls that have ties of silk cloth or plaited prayer flags, decorative hinges and straps embellish the massive doors. Doors are painted a deep red and sometimes also decorated with Buddhist patterns and motifs.

ABOVE:

Yama, who presides over the cycle of rebirth, grips the wheel of life in a painting at a temple entrance.

RIGHT FROM TOP:

Door pulls exhibit the fine artistry of Tibetan craftsmen. The finest door straps and pulls originally came from the town of Derge in Kham. Derge craftsmen used the damascene technique in which metals of contrasting colours (such as gold and silver) are inlaid into metals such as iron or steel.

Carved on this temple door is a *dorje*, the symbol of the thunderbolt that represents the strength and indestructibility of religious power.

Doors are primarily painted red, a sacred colour. They may be painted with motifs and patterns such as the popular *kati-rimo* pattern, a lattice design of flower medallions.

ASSEMBLY SPACE GRACED BY LIGHT

Temple interiors are usually brimming with decorative detail, as if representing the rich internal spiritual life of the monastic body and the nearby communities. Stepping into a temple you are struck by the richness of colour and pattern created by layers of textiles and paintings, the warmth of the predominant red colour, and the solemnity of the space marked by tall pillars. Where else in the world does one find such richly hued assembly halls, some with as many as 48 tall red pillars? The tallest pillars rise to a central skylight that sheds light over the otherwise windowless space.

The main assembly halls of Tibetan monasteries such as Drepung are examples of superb communal spaces. Long silk banners catch light from the skylight above, and bands of gentle light fall upon the rows of benches and tables where the monks perform their rituals. Around this ritual space worshippers circumambulate, visiting important shrines, making offerings, prostrating, and viewing with awe the thangkas and murals that cover the surfaces of the walls.

In the assembly hall of Tashilhunpo Monastery, Shigatse, silk cloth catches natural light as it filters from windows above.

The column bases at Tashilhunpo Monastery are painted with a rainbow, clouds, water, mountains, and other Tibetan motifs.

LEFT: Beams of daylight illuminate the magnificent Drepung Monastery assembly hall as monks recite prayers.

CAULDRONS OF BUTTER TEA

No monastery could survive without its large kitchens. Drepung Monastery is famous for its steaming cauldrons and smoke-darkened walls that are illuminated by shafts of daylight. Dozens of brass ladles are strung between two columns, while rows of copper pots and pitchers stored on wooden shelves are at the ready to be filled with steaming butter tea or rice. Cakes of tea, blocks of butter, and butter tea churns are also numerous to supply the need throughout the monastery for hot and nourishing refreshment.

CLOCKWISE FROM TOP: Copper pitchers and pots line long wooden shelves in Drepung's kitchen.

A painted cupboard in Drepung's kitchen stores butter tea containers hand-made with wood and brass. They are used by young monks who will dash from the kitchen to serve hot tea to the monks who chant in the assembly hall.

Monks make *torma* (ritual offering figures of barley flour and butter) in the monastery kitchen in Gansi, Eastern Tibet.

OPPOSITE:

Ladles strung between the smoke-darkened pillars of Drepung's giant kitchen.

TEXTILES: SPLENDOUR AND WARMTH

ABOVE: A decorated yak with colourful saddle carpets lies along the kora at Drak Yerpa Hermitage, Tibet.

OPPOSITE: Yak hair curtains protect a temple portico of Tashilhunpo Monastery from the elements. Steep steps have pole railings with brass casings.

Curtains appliquéd with images of deer and the wheel of life at Thupten Chöling Monastery, Solu, Nepal.

Monks sit on thick hand-woven carpets while reading prayers at Hemis Monastery, Ladakh.

Brocade cloth is used to mount thangka paintings, which are hung overlapping between cloth-wrapped temple pillars at Drak Yerpa.

Decorative, colourful and providing warmth or shade, textiles are integral to religious buildings. The value and significance of thangka paintings is emphasized by the expensive silk brocade on which they are mounted. Temple entrances and porches may be protected by immense door curtains of cotton or hand-woven yak hair, often appliquéd with auspicious Tibetan knots or two deer on either side of the wheel of dharma. The low benches on which monks chant and pray are softened by hand-woven carpets. Men in Tibet's Wangden Valley learned from a high lama how to weave runners and sitting carpets known as Wangden *drumtse*, which have thick pile and a shaggy fringe. Along the kora one may encounter animals whose decorations spread good fortune.

LADAKH RESTORES:
RELIGIOUS BUILDINGS, PALACES
AND NOBLE HOUSES

Located on key trading routes of South and Central Asia, for centuries the kingdom of Ladakh was host to peoples of different cultures who influenced the style of architecture, art, and crafts. It is recorded that 32 sculptors and wood carvers from Kashmir helped to build the monastery complex at Alchi. Alchi's famous three-storey temple (*Sumsteg*), dating from the 13th century, was exquisitely painted by Kashmiri artists. The wooden window screens built in traditional Ladhaki houses also owe their origins to Kashmir. Following the establishment of schools of Tibetan Buddhism in the 15th century, the architectural style of palaces and monasteries followed the style developed in Central Tibet. Newar sculptors and craftsmen from Nepal were brought to Ladakh to build the immense statue of Buddha in the 17th-century Shey Monastery. Today their descendants live in the town of Chilling, famous for its production of silver vessels.

Ladakh is now an autonomous region within the Indian state of Jammu and Kashmir, its dominant culture being Tibetan. Within the old town of Leh are nearly 200 historic buildings, most in need of repair. Unplanned development is coming fast to Leh and other Ladakhi towns, and so efforts to preserve Ladakh's unique identity are imperative. This chapter highlights projects preserving the traditional architecture of Ladakh.

Leh Palace, under restoration, looms above the town of Leh. The whitewashed exterior of Gompa Soma is seen below the palace to the right.

LEH PALACE

From its perch on a rocky hilltop, Leh Palace towers above the town of Leh. The impressive palace, now under restoration by the Archeological Survey of India (ASI), once expressed the power of King Senge Namgyal who ruled the kingdom of Ladakh from 1616 to 1642. We know that the designer of the Tibetan-style palace was in fact a Balti Muslim, known as Shinkar Chandan, or 'Carpenter Changan'. The nine-storey structure was at the time the largest building in Asia, predating the twelve-storey Potala in Lhasa. Much of its masonry has remained intact and shows the influence of Tibetan builders and building methods. Unique to Ladakhi buildings, however, is the popularity of the south-facing *rabsel*, or projecting balcony. Stacked rabsels were used in abundance on the upper south and east-facing walls.

Rooms above the strong stone foundations were once used by servants and for storage. The royal family inhabited the top level within walls built primarily of mud bricks made by hand in a wooden mold. Brick and earth walls were always set on a stone base to prevent water damage. Today the structure's walls, timberwork, and earthen floors and ceilings are undergoing a restoration process in keeping with local building traditions.

The original wooden entrance to the palace is distinctive in its construction and carved details. Its four columns, each composed of many slender wooden poles, are topped by finely carved brackets that support a roof with parapet. Above the door are three carved lion heads. It is said that in the past, when the door opened, the lion in the centre would pop out and roar, frightening visitors and asserting the king's power.

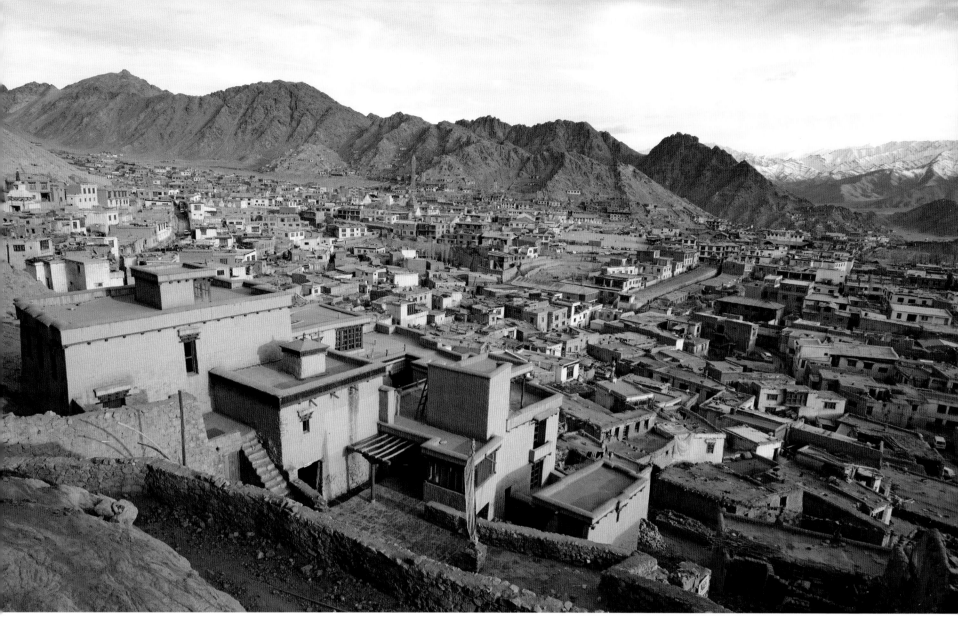

ABOVE: Munshi House was joined together with another private house named the Gyaoo House. The upper level of the Gyaoo House became the new entrance for the Ladakh Arts and Media Organization (LAMO). A salvaged beam and poplar joists were used to create a pergola.

RIGHT: Leh Palace, seen from the terrace of LAMO. In the foreground is the reading room, once the summer room of the Munshi family. Its row of south-facing double-glazed windows opens to the terrace.

OPPOSITE ABOVE: The central bay of the library room was left open and the roof raised to let in natural light. Floors were paved with slate brought from the town of Chilling on the Zanskar River.

OPPOSITE BELOW: View over the interconnecting terraces. Following tradition, terraces and rooftops were waterproofed with *markalak*, a chalk-like mineral with lime content that is mixed with earth.

MUNSHI HOUSE RESTORED

Those who served the king lived in houses descending the hill from the palace: here were the large houses of the ministers as well as the simpler houses of the cook, the dogkeeper, the royal tailor and others. Munshi House, the house of the king's secretary, has been superbly preserved by the Ladakh Arts and Media Organization (LAMO).

Utilizing stones found in the ruins and making mud bricks on site, the building was re-created under the expert guidance of architect John Harrison. The new library receives light through a restored balcony (rabsel) while a demolished summer room that the Munshi family had built in the mid-19th century was recreated with double-glazed windows to make a reading room. For paving, slate was brought from Chilling, a town on the Zanskar River. Parapets were faced with salvaged *burtse,* a mountain shrub now hard to find, and sticks of willow. The mud plaster applied to the exterior retains the imprints of the craftsmen's hands. Restored with respect to original design elements and materials, the building's rhythm of rooms and terraces looks contemporary. With space for exhibits, film screenings, and workshop projects that document and showcase Ladakhi culture, the revived and adapted Munshi House is a model for the region.

GOMPA SOMA

Under the guidance of the late German restoration expert André Alexander, the Tibet Heritage Fund (THF) initiated the Leh Old Town Conservation Programme, which identified historic structures in Leh for preservation. At Gompa Soma, built in the mid-1800s below Leh Palace, THF re-paved with slate the courtyard where dances and ceremonies are held during Ladakhi New Year celebrations. Also restored by THF was the courtyard's surrounding gallery with its graceful row of timber pillars and plastered walls with narrow windows.

RIGHT: Bright orange doors at the entry of Gompa Soma.

BELOW: The paved courtyard of Gompa Soma restored by THF, surrounded by a graceful timber gallery.

OPPOSITE CLOCKWISE:

The interior courtyard of LAMO, with its restored timberwork and parapet of brushwood. Stepping stones of slate were added to the earth and markalak floor surface. The library's south-facing rabsel with glass doors can be seen above.

Plaster relief of a wind horse on a stupa below Leh Palace.

The exterior walls of LAMO retain a rich hand-plastered texture.

The restoration of the citadel and temples of Basgo is an example
of a successful project initiated by a local community.

REVITALIZATION OF LADAKH'S TEMPLES

The extensive renovation of monasteries has not always pleased
conservationists; however, the energy dedicated to their rebuilding
points to the strength of Ladakhi religious devotion and pride. Ladakhis
are fortunate that the Tibetan Buddhist religion thrives in Ladakh
without the devastating interference suffered in Tibet. The tradition of
religious statue-making, too, remains vigorous.

One of the finest examples of temple restoration can be seen in the
village of Basgo. The walls, citadel and mud-brick temples of Basgo,
dating from the 16th century, cluster dramatically on a hilltop in a dry
pink and grey landscape. The complex was restored on the initiative of
the Basgo community and with the support of the World Monuments
Fund. As you climb the steps you note careful use of materials: the steps
are made of rock rather than cement and the retaining walls employ

traditional methods of stone masonry with wooden tie beams. The
UNESCO Asia Pacific Award of Excellence, the highest award for
heritage conservation in the region, was awarded to the Basgo village
community for its restoration of three temples in this historic site.
With their colourful painted walls and ceilings, wooden columns and
floors, Basgo's Maitreya temples are a delight to behold. The Maitreya is
the fifth Buddha, the Buddha of the future, whose image, when looked
upon, brings merit and inspires hope: the Maitreya will liberate all
beings and lead them to an eternal state of bliss. The centuries-old gilt
copper Maitreya statue created by Nepalese craftsmen maintains a
powerful presence in the Serzang Temple, while in the Chamba Temple
the head of the 14-metre high clay Maitreya extends well-above the
main ceiling.

This stupa (probably dating from 1100 AD) with a distinctive mandala-shaped dome is situated along the entrance path to the Basgo citadel.

Ladakh's largest clay figure, a 15-metre Maitreya stands in a hall in the striking hilltop Thiksey Gompa. Created by the Ladakhi artist Nawang Tsering, this impressive statue has become an icon for modern Ladakh and has been included in the scenes of feature films. Its gilded countenance, peaceful and all-knowing, as well as its colourful crown and jewels and its enormous hands in a graceful *mudra*, inspire joy and confidence. When consecrating the statue, His Holiness the Dalai Lama told the Thiksey Rinpoche, "This Maitreya is very beautiful. Even if you see this Maitreya again and again you will never see it enough: you will always want to see it more – you will never be satisfied."

The Dolma Lhakhang in Spituk Monastery exemplifies the colour and vitality common to Tibetan temple interiors. Here 21 gilt copper Tara (or Dolma) statues brought from Tibet by His Holiness the Dalai Lama are enshrined in a cabinet intensely decorated with images of dragons and peonies. The room with its orange walls glows warmly. A framed portrait of Most Venerable Kushok Bakula, the great lama of Ladakh, hangs above a painted wooden couch.

Bakula was named 'the Architect of Modern Ladakh' for his advocacy of both education and preservation of Ladakhi culture. We visited his six-year-old reincarnation, Thubstan Nawang, and after giving us blessings, the enchanting young Rinpoche displayed his skill riding a brand new bike with training wheels.

ABOVE:

The 14-metre high gilded Maitreya statue in Serzang Lhakhang, Basgo, was created by Nepalese artisans in the 16th century.

LEFT:

Painted patterns on the ceiling beams of the Chamba Lhakhang at Basgo. Careful documentation and condition assessment prior to the restoration of the Lhakhang's paintings was carried out by the Namgyal Institute for Research in Ladakhi Art and Culture.

A RINPOCHE FOUNDS A SCHOOL

Past a field of chortens below Shey Palace, a number of low stone buildings sit peaceably in the dry valley landscape. The flat-roofed buildings are arranged as if in a monastery or village, facing onto large open courtyards. From a distance you might not know that the placement of nine buildings forms a mandala, and that this mandala is the Druk White Lotus School. Founded by Ladakhi spiritual leader, the 12th Gyalwang Drukpa, it is supported by the Drukpa Trust under the patronage of His Holiness the Dalai Lama. Some of the children come from local villages while others from far away. 200 of the 628 are on scholarships and 260 live in school dormitories. During morning assemblies the children recite the prayers they learn from a lama, and each year they prepare for their Ladakhi festival, with different classes competing in presentations of Ladakhi food, dress, nomadic life, and other aspects of the culture they will help to preserve.

Construction has been managed by Arup Associates, which each year gives a leave of absence to a member of its engineering or architecture team to work with the school. The school has won World Architecture Awards for the Best Educational Building in Asia, and the Best Educational Building in the World. For its unique dry pit toilets with a cooling system it received the Best Green Building in Asia award.

The exterior walls are built with local granite, mud mortar, and cement pointing. The timber for the wooden frames and doors is sourced not far away, the ceilings are made following local style with willow sticks – the willow is provided by monastery plantations nearby. Solar panels provide electricity for lights and computers, and windows with double layers of glass allow for passive solar heating.

Through the open spaces of the circular assembly area spectacular mountain views are framed like paintings. One day, stupas will be erected around the classroom buildings and people will follow a circumambulation path that includes a nearby monastery. The school complex illustrates the links between tradition, environment, and development and clearly marks a new direction for local design and technology.

CLOCKWISE FROM TOP:

The dark south-facing facade helps heat and drive air up a solar flue of the solar-assisted VIP (ventilated improved pit) latrine.

Single-storey buildings made of local materials open onto landscaped courtyards.

The southern walls are formed of timber-framed windows and pillars supporting solar panels.

OPPOSITE CLOCKWISE:

The amphitheater is located at the centre of the mandala layout of the school complex.

For the classrooms, local building styles and materials, such as poplar and willow ceilings, are combined with modern solar technology.

The elevated roof above the kindergarten room allows for a band of windows that let in additional natural light.

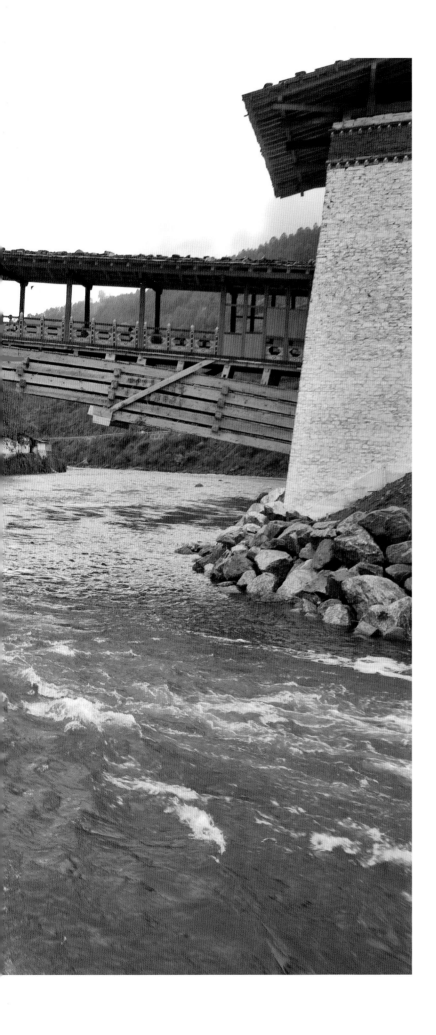

DZONGS AND LHAKHANGS IN BHUTAN

In the ancient past, the word *dzong* may have referred to a power place that could be simply a sacred rock or cave. Gradually temples were built on these points, which over time needed protection through fortification. Today's dzongs are connected to these power places and have been erected in strategic locations above the confluence of rivers with commanding views all around.

The architecture of Bhutan's extraordinary dzongs is closely related to the early *khar* architecture of Tibet. Khars were fortified tower palaces built by Tibet's ruling aristocrats. In the 14th century Tibet was divided into districts, with the district rulers governing from fortresses called dzongs. Tibet's dzongs were largely destroyed in the Cultural Revolution, but dzongs are still prominent in Bhutan.

In the 17th century, the great first ruler of Bhutan, Ngawang Namgyel (known popularly as the Zhabdrung) established dzongs in order to control and protect Bhutan's districts. The Zhabdrung originated a uniquely Bhutanese style of dzong. Serving both administrative and monastic purposes, and thereby representing the harmony of sacred and secular life, each dzong contained a tower called an utse, which like a khar, was designed for defense. To increase surveillance and protection for the dzong, a *taa dzong*, or watchtower was erected nearby.

Within dzongs are numerous lhakhangs or temples. Lhakhangs may also be in separate buildings or incorporated in monasteries. Religious buildings are identified by their dark orange or red painted band that in Bhutan is called a *kemar* band (meaning 'red neck') and their golden roof spires.

The interchange of building design and expertise in the Himalayas is exemplified in the construction of the early Bhutanese dzongs. The Zhabdrung's first dzong, Simtokha, was started in 1639 with help from Tibetan monks who had left Tibet. They built the 70 x 60 metre dzong in the symmetrical form of a mandala. Punakha Dzong, the Zhabdrung's second dzong, was designed by a famous Tibetan architect and housed a college of Tibetan scholars. In 1753, when the tower of the Punakha Dzong was rebuilt with a new golden roof, the effort involved a great many craftsmen from Nepal.

The massive cantilevered bridge over the Mo River at Punakha Dzong was rebuilt through the support of the philanthropic association, Pro Bhutan. The original 17th-century bridge that was washed away in 1958 had a span of 35 feet. The new one, spanning 55 feet due to the widening of the river, is reinforced with steel.

WITHIN A LHAKHANG

As you take off your shoes a monk unlocks the door to a semi-dark intimate space that you feel privileged to enter. A lhakhang in Bhutan, each like a small museum, is unique in its details, depictions, and treasures. The walls may be covered with religious paintings, as thangka artists paint religious murals on large canvases that are later applied to the walls. You cross a floor of polished wood to visit the altar. Fine statues of clay, thangka paintings, and other sacred items of worship gradually come into focus as you light your butter lamps. The monk introduces each statue of a deity as if it were an old friend, then pours into your hand holy water that is cold and is flavoured by camphor wood and coloured orange by saffron.

CLOCKWISE FROM LEFT:

At Jampa Lhakhang, Bumthang, a large square chorten is topped by a golden spire.

A monk crosses in front of a monastic school (Tshedra) near Gangtey Gompa. Large white circles painted on the wall's deep orange (kemar) band suggest mirrors. Small white circles are a common motif that mimics the ends of joists.

The gilded copper disk (melong) on the kemar band at Jampa Lhakhang.

A small lhakhang in eastern Bhutan seems to float on its surrounding stone pavement.

Offerings called *tsa tsa* are placed on window ledges at Jampa Lhakhang.

Below a protector chapel of Wangdi Dzong, a young monk looks out from an arched window.

ABOVE:

Silk banners and a scarf (*kata*) hide a protector chapel.

RIGHT:

Brass offering bowls are lined on a table in a lhakhang in Bumthang.

OPPOSITE CLOCKWISE:

Butter lamp offerings on an altar table.

Incense sticks in offering bowls filled with rice.

Two men cross a courtyard of Trongsa Dzong toward the painted portico of a lhakhang. Over their *gho* (men's robe) they wear a *kabney*, a raw silk scarf that is required when visiting a dzong. It is worn from left shoulder to right hip.

Monks cross through a passageway, lit by simple open windows, that links the buildings of Trongsa Dzong.

DETAILS OF THE INTERIOR FAÇADE

Facing onto interior courtyards, and contrasting with the strong stone outer walls of the dzong, are façades with various carved and painted timber details. Some window shapes follow the Tibetan style with elaborate tablature above, while others are small and arched, usually in rows of three or four. Window openings extending outward from the building, with or without balconies, are called rabsels. Colours of window frames and other timber elements such as railings, columns, and brackets are predominantly dark red and grey, contrasting with the white plastered walls.

ABOVE: The 50-metre high semi-circular tower (utse) of Jakar Dzong.

TOP RIGHT: Three stacked painted wooden balconies (rabsels) at Trashigang Dzong, eastern Bhutan.

LOWER RIGHT: Narrow Tibetan-style windows at Jakar Dzong bordered in grey.

FAR RIGHT: View across Wangdi Dzong's paved courtyard. Tragically, Wangdi Dzong burned down in 2012.

TRONGSA DZONG

For several years I enjoyed a view of Trongsa Dzong from my window. I watched it disappear in banks of Trongsa's heavy mist and then reappear magically, first the roofs and spires and then the elegant white walls. To me it was more than a magnificent example of dzong architecture, yet how does one describe a structure that seems to be as elemental as the rock cliff it was built upon? Its tall angled walls seem to rise out of the earth; its roofs seem to settle over the walls as naturally as a flock of birds. The bold maroon painted band that in Bhutan is called a kemar band runs like a rich vein below the roofs, bestowing the whitewashed walls with power and resonance.

Considered to be the most impressive of Bhutanese dzongs, Trongsa Dzong has been extended over time. It has several courtyards linked by stone steps and passageways. In these carefully paved courtyards I've attended Buddhist rituals or Cham dances that are performed unhurriedly over periods of days in honour of Guru Rinpoche. With its murals in the entry-ways to lhakhangs and painted wood balconies, rabsels and staircases, the interior space is surprisingly light and colourful in contrast to the more fortress-like exterior.

Seen from the hillside above, you appreciate how its successive buildings join in easy rhythm, each protected by a different roof. The roofs of Trongsa Dzong shelter hundreds of monks, administration offices, and twenty-seven temples. From the watch tower, Taa Dzong, that sits on a hill above the dzong, you can count the intersecting planes and gold spires of Trongsa Dzong's red roofs. A lhakhang may be designated by a *serthog* (a pinnacle that is stupa-shaped) or a *gyaltshen or gyeltsen* (victory banner).

Trongsa Dzong's monastic buildings to the right and administrative buildings to the left have been conjoined and extended over time. Façades facing the courtyard are more detailed than outer façades and have elaborate painted wooden balconies and windows. Like many of Bhutan's buildings, the Dzong has made the transition from traditional shingle roofs to roofs made of corrugated metal.

Gilded spires indicate the location of lhakhangs within Trongsa Dzong. The Dzong was strategically built on a ridgetop above the Mangdi Chhu Valley.

The paved main courtyard of Trongsa Dzong with interconnected administrative and religious buildings. Painted timber brackets, rabsels, and balconies contrast with whitewashed stone wall surfaces.

Spiritual texts are wrapped in orange cloth between two wooden book covers. Colourful squares of cloth are inscribed with a sequence number. The books are carefully stored in painted bookcases.

The main door to Trongsa Dzong opens onto a row of prayer wheels behind arched openings.

A principal feature of the façade, a projecting window or balcony, is called a rabsel or *rabsey* (meaning clear or best light). In Tibetan temples, the rabsel is set above the portico and provides a sunny place for senior monks to sit. In Bhutan, where timber is less scarce, rabsels can be multi-tiered, creating a striking artistic feature that is found on both monastic and secular buildings.

In the evening, after the dzong has descended into shadow, Taa Dzong holds the late light, glowing white against the dark greenery of its perch. For several years, while my husband managed a project for its restoration, I observed how Taa Dzong was transformed from a ruin into a spectacular museum.

LEFT:

The highest level of Buddhist philosophy is represented in Gallery 11 at the top of the central tower. A stupa representing full perfection is dramatically suspended by cables in the tower's central opening.

OPPOSITE:

The Taa Dzong, comprised of a central five-storey tower and north and south wings, has been converted into the Tower of Trongsa Museum.

THE TOWER OF TRONGSA

Taa Dzong in Trongsa was the first major building in Bhutan to undergo a renovation that brings new architectural concepts to an otherwise preserved traditional space. Built in 1652, Taa Dzong sits on a steep hill overlooking Trongsa Dzong and the river valleys to the south and west. During times of war and intrigue, it was traditional to build such watchtowers to protect a dzong. In more recent times, Taa Dzong had become home to two hermit monks who tended the two lhakhangs inside. Now a museum of Buddhism and the monarchy named the 'Tower of Trongsa', it still shelters two active lhakhangs. Götz Hagmüller, a renowned Viennese architect, created the designs for Taa Dzong's transformation. Viennese experts worked closely with a Bhutanese construction team and curator Dorji Namgyel to create Bhutan's most innovative restoration project to date.

Taa Dzong's five-storey central tower (*utse*) is topped with a circular roof reminiscent of the popular Bhutanese bamboo hat. The utse is connected to two other massive towers by side wings that were likely constructed later. Today the south wing houses the administrative headquarters of the museum as well as rooms for the hermit monks who live at Taa Dzong. The north wing and the central utse have been converted into museum space.

A distinctive feature of the museum design is that you move from gallery to gallery with a sense of anticipation. How will you find your way through the tower to its lookout point? The journey is one of discovery as you explore the eleven galleries, eventually reaching the top terrace with a panoramic view of the distant snow-capped Black Mountains. The ascent through the museum is meant to evoke the path to enlightenment, and certainly your impression, after a last winding stair, is that you have reached a supreme destination.

The journey begins at a traditionally built stone gate below the Taa Dzong. A long climb up stone steps fringed by ferns brings you to tall prayer flags gracing the museum's entrance in the north tower. After entering, you immediately mount a wooden staircase to a solemn circular space that feels sacred. Light glows from within silk temple banners that hang from above, while around you are the lit sculptures of the four guardian kings who ward off evil from the four cardinal directions – guardians customarily present at the entry of a Bhutanese temple.

A second staircase leads further up the tower to Gallery 2, devoted to local deities and legends, and Gallery 3 that contains the famed 'Raven Crown' of the Bhutanese monarchy. Here at the top of the north tower is a power point. The dagger-shaped showcase for the crown is painted red and points downwards to a shiny cast brass tile. Götz's design aptly captures the sacred power and energy that infuses those who wear the royal crown.

ABOVE:

A clay sculpture of Chakrasamvara is displayed in Gallery 3. Traditionally, the making of clay sculptures involves special rituals and use of materials, such as clay brought from different locations in Bhutan and blessed by high lamas.

LEFT:

The dynamic display case for the Raven Crown, pointing to a brass pyramid embedded in the floor.

OPPOSITE:

Gallery 8 on the first floor of the tower displays clay sculptures representing Guru Rinpoche, the 8th-century Indian mystic who introduced Buddhism to Tibet, and his eight manifestations. The Guru is placed in a niche that used to be a loophole used for shooting arrows. Butter lamps are lit before him.

Windows and balconies (whose original purpose was for dropping stones on attackers) allow spectacular views over Trongsa Dzong and the Mangdi Chhu Valley. Interior timber elements are stained a medium brown, and the floors after staining are polished with red-tinted wax. Walls are painted a natural pale mud colour. Simple open stairways with an easy gradient have unobtrusively replaced the more traditional steep ladder steps.

Few objects are placed in the centre of the room so as to maintain an impression of openness in the generally simple galleries. Clay sculptures are displayed without showcases, and local visitors worship these deities as they would in a temple. Main gallery texts are printed on fabric and hung on the walls like scrolls. Gilded frames protect flat objects (textiles and paper) and hang at a little distance from the walls so that they appear to float outwards. Some objects are enclosed in cases within the niches created by the buildings' original loopholes, while other sculptures and objects sit on pedestals that extend from the walls like buttresses.

Entering the solemn Gallery 8 in the utse, you are surrounded by eight lit manifestations of Guru Rinpoche, the 8th-century Indian mystic who spread Buddhism in Tibet. Set on pedestals on a semi-circular rise, the statues throw unearthly shadows on the curved walls behind them. Further up in the tower you discover the most daring feature of the museum's spatial design: wide circular openings in the upper two floors allow a central shaft of daylight to fall gradually down into the building for the illumination of Galleries 10 and 11. "Given this natural skylight from above," Götz explains, "the display concept for the deities and ritual objects with the utse follows the ascending order of Buddhist imagery – from the nether to the upper and transcending realms – and correlates with the visitor's ascent from the darker levels below to increasingly light ones above."

In Gallery 10, the five Tathagata Buddhas of Mahayana Buddhism are placed on an octagonal pedestal, four of them facing the cardinal directions, and the fifth one raised on the central vertical axis. Looking down the circular opening from the topmost Gallery 11, the five lively coloured statues appear almost kaleidoscopic. But what is breathtaking on this level is a precious silver-plated and gilt votive stupa seemingly floating, as if on the Primordial Ocean, in the centre of the circular void. Although suspended on visible cables, the sight of the chorten in mid-air is magical, and once more attests to the bold genius behind the transformation of this historical structure.

RESTORATION OF A ROYAL SQUARE IN NEPAL

The Newar people, the dominant settlers of the Kathmandu Valley, share a distinct language and cultural identity. Although they consider themselves either Hindu or Buddhist, they worship the gods of both religions. The rhythm of Newar life is marked by unique life-cycle rituals as well as festivals that bring forth the gods through music and masked dance. Over the centuries, the Newars have played a seminal role in the development of Tibetan and Bhutanese art and architecture. At the same time, a distinct aesthetic developed within Newar towns of the Kathmandu Valley, influenced by India from the south and Tibet and China in the north.

It was the Malla kings, rulers from the 12th to the 18th centuries, who developed the sophisticated urban spaces in the three kingdoms in the Valley: Patan, Bhaktapur, and Kathmandu. Under the patronage of the Mallas, Newar painting, wood carving, stone carving, and metal arts flourished. The dynasty left behind well-laid out public squares with fine palaces and multi-tiered temples. These squares lie today within the Valley's seven Monument Zones that are listed together as a single UNESCO World Heritage Site.

The Patan Darbar Square, brick-paved and closed to traffic, inspires awe each time you enter this unique space. The square includes a 17th-century royal palace complex, step-well, and exquisite temples. There are three palaces in the complex, two of which (Mul Chowk and Sundari Chowk) are currently under restoration by the Kathmandu Valley Preservation Trust. The third palace, Keshav Narayan Chowk, lies on the north end of the square and houses the famed Patan Museum. The museum's seven main galleries are devoted to an elucidation of Hindu and Buddhist religion and antiquities. The museum also contains an exhibit on the metalwork techniques practiced by highly skilled Newar craftspeople who live and work in neighbourhoods nearby. In recent years, the royal complex has hosted a range of contemporary arts events, from concerts by local jazz and rock musicians to art installations by Nepalese and international artists participating in the Kathmandu International Arts Festival.

Patan Darbar Square with the royal palaces of the Malla kings who reigned till 1768. This view highlights the unique style of Nepal's multi-tiered temples. The temples were heavily damaged by the 1934 earthquake and were later rebuilt according to their original configurations. Ongoing restoration efforts have also recreated the square's historic brick pavement, preserved the palaces and repaired magnificent stone carvings and metal statues within the royal complex. The Sundari Chowk Palace in the foreground is currently under restoration by the Kathmandu Valley Preservation Trust. The roofs are being brought back to their original shape by employing heavy timber framing that is covered with original terracotta tiles laid in mud.

71

ABOVE: Keshav Narayan Chowk, a former residential palace of the Malla kings and now the Patan Museum, was created by King Vishnu Malla in 1734. Its wooden portal was clad in gilt copper in 1854. Known as 'the Golden Door' it exhibits superb three-dimensional work in repoussé. The palace's door, with a *torana* or tympanum installed above, resembles the entryway to a temple.

RIGHT: This exquisitely carved wooden strut depicts a demi-goddess who grasps a branch of a *sal* tree. A parrot, a symbol of love, balances on her left hand. The figure is known as a *salabhanjika*, or goddess of the sacred grove. The strut supports a roof of gilt copper in Uku Bahal. Much of the woodcarving seen on historic Kathmandu Valley buildings dates from the Malla period (12th to 18th centuries) but carbon-dating of Uku Bahal's struts suggests that at least some of the struts were carved between 690-890 AD by a superb craftsman who took care not only with the carving of the features and ornaments of the deity, but also with the natural elements framing them.

ABOVE: Hands of a statue in Uku Bahal, a revered Newar Monastery and Buddhist institution in Patan, exhibit the extraordinary quality of Newar metal craft. Metal arts date from the 7th century and still today some of the world's finest lost-wax casting and repoussé is produced in Patan's workshops. The creation of a statue involves the expertise of several craftsmen who divide the tasks of creating the wax model, casting, chasing, and gilding.

RIGHT: Detail of a stone relief carving in Tusha Hiti, the royal step-well in Sundari Chowk, Patan Darbar. The walls of Tusha Hiti, built in 1647 AD, are comprised of two rows of niches housing images of tantric deities. Stone carving is a two-thousand year-old tradition in the Kathmandu Valley, continued today by skilled master stone carvers who have retained detailed knowledge about design and proportion.

ART AND CRAFTSMANSHIP ON THE PATAN DARBAR

The Patan Darbar's Royal Palace Complex is alive with contemporary music performances and art exhibits, as well as ongoing restoration work undertaken by the Kathmandu Valley Preservation Trust (KVPT), an American INGO with local headquarters on the square. Within the courtyard of Mul Chowk one may glimpse the age-old activities of the Valley's craftspeople who have joined hands with experts and students from Vienna's University of Applied Arts to bring the palace back to its original glory. Six master metal craftsmen, including renowned lost-wax cast masters Rajan Shakya and Bijaya Ratna Shakya, have volunteered their skills to replace stolen figures in the torana above the golden door, which, along with the statues of the river goddesses Ganga and Yamuna, is undergoing extensive repair and regilding.

In the adjacent palace, Sundari Chowk, the Trust recently restored the magnificent Tusha Hiti. A hiti is a Newar step-well with one or more jutting stone spouts that are often carved in the form of a *makara*, a mythical water creature. The Trust disassembled the Tusha Hiti's 72 stone sculptures, created a damp-proof barrier to protect them from water in the ground, cleaned each of the sculptures and re-set them. They also commissioned Patan's masters of lost-wax casting to replace a stolen gilt-copper water spout.

During the restoration process we visited Bishwo Rathor in his workroom that is not more than 8 feet square. Moving carefully around the small wax arms, heads or torsos that lay upon the floor waiting to be cast, soldered, carved and polished, we documented how he was able to recreate the images of stolen deities. Some weeks later, a gilded Vishnu and Lakshmi on Garuda were remounted on the Tusha Hiti's spout. Witnessing how the beautiful Tusha Hiti was thus completed, we Patan residents rejoiced.

CLOCKWISE:

The river goddess Yamuna, with restored gilding and jewellery.

Ornamented deities on a carved window bracket in Mul Chowk.

Details of stone carvings on the water tank in the Bhandarkhal garden. Stones carved with naturalistic scenes depicting animals and trees are bordered with narrower stones with lotus and other decorative motifs.

OPPOSITE:

The golden doorway of the Taleju Temple in Mul Chowk is flanked by the gilt copper repoussé statues of Ganga and Yamuna, the goddesses associated with Hinduism's most sacred rivers. Local master metal craftsmen are helping KVPT to restore the entire golden door ensemble, along with conservation students from the University of Vienna.

PATAN DARBAR'S WATER ARCHITECTURE

For hundreds of years, step-wells and water tanks in the old city of Patan have been fed by a network of underground water channels. Considered sacred, these community water sources were fitted with stone and metal images of deities and mythological creatures. The artfulness of the stone carving, the design of gilded spouts, and features such as dedicatory inscriptions, have made this water architecture of tremendous historical and cultural importance.

The 17th-century Malla King Siddhinarasimha built the Bhandarkhal Tank in the garden of his new palace, Sundari Chowk, in order to honour his tutelary Taleju, the 'giver of existence', who had empowered previous kings to build their Valley kingdoms. On the side of the tank is a carved wooden pavilion and in the centre a golden lotus. It is said that the king gathered lotuses from the pond to offer to Taleju.

The Tusha Hiti was probably used for royal ablutions. Facing the opening is a large stone slab upon which the devout King Siddhinarasimha would sit to meditate and compose poetry.

ABOVE:

A woman collects water in the Tusha Hiti, the exquisite oval step-well in the courtyard of Sundari Chowk. 72 finely carved stone plaques line the step-well.

OPPOSITE CLOCKWISE:

Artist Bishwo Rathor works on a wax model in his Patan workshop.

Vishnu and Lakshmi on Garuda, mounted on the Tusha Hiti spout. The spout was recreated by Bishwo Rathor after the original spout was stolen.

A row of stone spouts at Dwarika's hotel were inspired by the traditional spouts of Patan. The spouts were carved by mastercraftsman Jaya Raj Bajracharya.

The Bhandarkhal Tank behind Mul Chowk, under restoration by KVPT. The trust restored the stone work of the tank and rebuilt a lost wooden pavilion.

THE PATAN MUSEUM

The Patan Museum is a second home to those who seek an urban oasis.
Within the museum there are numerous places for reflection and
repose – it is possible to spend a whole day there, perhaps first reading
the *Kathmandu Post* with a cappuccino in the outdoor café and then
moving to the exquisite halls upstairs. On each visit you learn anew
from exhibits that explain the history of stupas and mandalas,
important Hindu and Buddhist deities, lost wax casting and much
more. But the museum's open windows and cushioned window seats
also invite you to linger and gaze outwards, following the colourful
flow of people to temples on the great square below, or to simply
meditate quietly in the pleasant company of the galleries' deities.

You enter the museum through an exquisite 'golden door' on the
Darbar Square, and pass into a large courtyard at the centre of which is
a temple. The entry into the museum is a true passage. You leave the
bustling world of vendors, worshippers and pigeons on the great square
behind, and are provided a 'breathing space' in this open courtyard
before the museum experience begins.

The access to the galleries is located in the rear of the building, in
the east wing that faces the café and garden area. It was this wing that
had been poorly restored after the earthquake of 1934 and was in need
of complete rebuilding when the museum project was begun in the
mid-1980s.

ABOVE: The Patan Darbar Square, with the Patan Museum on the left
and the adjacent three-tiered Degutale Temple. A pillar with Garuda
stands on the right. Vehicle traffic has been forbidden on the square,
preserving its historical integrity and allowing an undisturbed
experience of its monuments.

LEFT: The main courtyard of the Patan Museum, into which the
visitor enters from the Darbar Square. Within the courtyard is a small
domed shrine to Vishnu. The museum's external walkway is formed by
a balcony with struts supporting the roof.

Seeking a new façade for the rear of the east wing, architect Götz Hagmüller was acutely aware of the UNESCO 1964 Charter of Venice requiring new construction to be built in the 'spirit of the time' rather than attempting to recreate and reproduce 'by conjecture' the original structure. Since there was no historical evidence of what the original façade once looked like, the architect was free to recreate the appearance and structure of the east wing. Götz made a number of characteristically inventive decisions.

The new façade was inspired by the style popular in Nepal under Rana rule (1845-1951), with exposed bricks and contrasting white plaster window trim and details. But then Götz merged a post-modern element, the curved balcony windows, with the Rana-era façade. As dissimilar to Rana style as the windows may be, they remain balanced and graceful. Such departures from tradition are not intended to shock, but to respond to the essential form and spirit of the building. Moreover they are purposeful: the balcony windows allow for greater light for the stairwells and surrounding display.

A second major decision was to reproduce traditional carved wooden pillars in steel. The use of steel is repeated in the roof structure of the east wing. For these exposed steel elements the architect drew criticism from strict conservationists, and applause from those who appreciated his personal and imaginative approach to conservation and museum design.

To reach the galleries on the first and second floors, you climb a new stairway inspired by the temple stairways of Tibet. The long poles that serve as handrails have typical Tibetan brass casings at each end. The stairs at the entrance are not purely for getting to the galleries – they are also used for closer viewing of elaborately carved roof struts that a viewer could otherwise not have access to.

Götz speaks of his love of the thick traditional walls, for such walls allow for the possibility to sculpt, play, and interact. It is here that the objects nestle in niches or appear, as if self-emanating, on inbuilt pedestals. The historic walls of the long galleries become the vehicle for illuminating the storey.

Many of the objects displayed in the museum had once been rescued from art thieves but then were doomed to be hidden in the dark storerooms of the palace for many years. In re-introducing 200 objects to the public, Götz needed to consider: were they still objects of worship or were they works of art? The decision to place mirrors under some objects so that they reflect the showcase light also from below was intended to create the effect of butter lamps lit in reverence to the deities of the statues. Generally, stone sculptures are not enclosed in cases and today it is common to see visitors bow their heads and softly touch them. Thus the objects retain a dual identity – they are both sacred objects to be worshipped, and objects to be admired for their aesthetic beauty.

Apart from showcase light, the rooms rely on natural light for illumination. Gentle light plays through new small window openings or through the traditional lattice windows that make intricate patterns on the polished tile floors. In the east wing, windows in a horizontal band under the roof allow for just enough light to enter the room, without diminishing the effect of the lighting designed specially for each object.

Traditional mud floors have been replaced by terracotta tiles and inessential partition walls have been removed. The sanctuary created by practical changes coupled with Götz Hagmüller's aesthetic, is cool, calm, even seductive. You enter the museum and hesitate to leave. Before returning to the bustling world, you can take a stroll through an organic garden, or enjoy a *dhal bhat* served on a brass plate in the outdoor café. Should it be a rainy day, you take a table under a tiled roof supported by carved columns – here the architect has taken inspiration from the *pati*, the traditional public resting place built in Newar villages and towns and along routes for trade.

RIGHT: In an installation by Saurganga Darshandari during the Kathmandu International Art Festival, pairs of plaster of paris feet step outward from the Narayan Temple in the courtyard of the Patan Museum.

OPPOSITE CLOCKWISE:

The reconstruction of the east-wing façade maintains the neoclassical style of the Rana period. The new bay window allows light into the stairwell, while other windows were closed to limit external light or to serve as display alcoves. The Shiva lingam in the foreground is revered daily with fresh flowers.

Pairs of pillars in the main courtyard's northern arcade. Only the upper sections of the columns are intensely carved. Niches carved in the top of the pillars hold seated or dancing female figures.

Steel pillars and brackets of the new arcade at the east-wing entrance to the Patan Museum are the architect's re-interpretation of carved wood columns common in the Kathmandu Valley. Wood encloses some of the steel structure of the columns.

CLOCKWISE:

At the entry to the galleries, a bronze donor figure dating from 1870 AD greets visitors with a *namaste*. It is displayed within a terracotta niche and a torana (tympanum), which were found in the museum's garden and were probably the remains of temples destroyed during the 1934 earthquake.

The four-faced stone lingam is displayed in a gallery dedicated to Lord Shiva. As its original base was lost it was placed on a contemporary angular *yoni* and displayed on a pedestal that allows the visitor to appreciate it at eye-level.

Bronze ritual objects are displayed in lit niches in the museum's exit stairwell.

ABOVE:

In the galleries, the warm wall colour blends with terracotta tiles and dark wood. Lattice windows let in natural light. Stone sculptures are left unenclosed so that they may be touched and revered as they would be in a temple.

RIGHT:

The gilt copper repoussé throne dating from 1666 was used by Patan's Malla kings for more than a hundred years. Elephants and lions support the throne, behind which are nine intertwined *nagas* (protective serpents). Beneath the seat is a Garuda, the mount of the god Vishnu. An inscription below the seat reads: "Anybody can hire this throne on payment of two rupees to the families of coppersmith and carpenter. Let it be auspicious."

ABOVE:

The openness of the main Buddhist gallery allows for a long view to the adjoining wing. Left exposed are the steel trusses of the roof. Indirect daylight is allowed to enter through a space between the roof and walls.

LEFT:

A case displaying unusual figures of deities perhaps produced by blacksmiths in hill communities. Showcases are built of simple handmade steel sections that are welded and screwed together, and are designed specially to give each object its own space, distinctive from its neighbour's. Local reflector bulbs are used to provide illumination from above.

ABOVE:

From comfortable seats by windows on the top floor, visitors can relax and gaze out over the Patan Darbar Square. The replica of a finial (*gajura*) from a Bhaktapur temple was made in Patan using the technique of repoussé. Gilded copper gajuras on the tops of temples and shrines symbolically link man to the universe.

RIGHT:

A niche above a lattice window was transformed into a showcase in the Technology Gallery. A hidden lightbox above illuminates bronze hands created by the lost-wax cast process. The hands may have belonged to an image of the Shakyamuni Buddha. They are displayed in the gesture of 'calling the earth to witness'.

ABOVE:

In the café, a secluded table sits beside a wall of niches under a roof supported by contemporary columns with decorative brass bases.

OPPOSITE CLOCKWISE:

The restoration project repaired an ancient paved courtyard, using patterns of brick traditional in the Kathmandu Valley and adding Hagmüller's own stone oil lamp design.

A covered seating area resembles a traditional *pati,* or resthouse for pilgrims.

Wooden seats are installed on a square brick and tile planter, with stone receptacles for oil lamps inserted at each corner.

Glazed ceramic tiles made in Bhaktapur add a decorative element to the terracotta tile tables. The patterns of tiles were inspired by Nepalese board games.

PART 2

DESIGN AND DEVOTION

The vernacular homes and spiritual structures of Himalayan peoples often settle so harmoniously into the surrounding environment that they appear to belong there. Where there are traditional settlements, in hills or valleys, people have propitiated mountain, water and other spirits of the cosmos to grant them permission to build, farm and benefit from the resources of their environment.

With the same cosmic awareness, religious monuments are erected at auspicious places in a town or landscape. During the construction of a stupa, for example, a spiritual teacher advises on its placement and its form as well as the treasures that are put inside. There are eight basic forms of stupas that refer to events in the Buddha's life. In general, however, the shapes of stupas are innumerable in colour, form, size, and design and are often changed over time by the elements.

Images representing deities and their holy energies, interpreted by different artisans and artists, are blessed with flowers, lights and other offerings. Spiritual offerings are made following religious custom, and at the same time they are infinite in their arrangements and compositions.

Profound in religious meaning and purpose, a statue of a god or a lingam is a god to believers, indivisible from its artistry. This chapter presents distinctive forms of buildings and objects of devotion as well as the aesthetic inherent in activities of prayer and worship.

A stupa catches late light in Tholing, capital of the ancient Guge Kingdom, western Tibet.

Monks circumambulate the dome of Bouddhanath stupa, Kathmandu, where oil lights glow in low niches. The eyes of Vairochana, the Great Illuminator, look out from the *harmika* above.

OPPOSITE:

Stupas built on a ridge at Drak Yerpa, Tibet. A central stupa is surrounded by smaller ones on a raised rectangular platform.

THE STUPA

A stupa, *chaitya* (Nepal) or *chorten* (Tibet) is the chief architectural object of Buddhist worship and is the focal point for religious activities. Circumambulation of a stupa helps you to achieve merit and just the view of the stupa encourages you to seek enlightenment. Buddhists walk clockwise, usually turning prayer wheels that are at the base of the stupa.

A stupa contains votives of similar shape (*tsa-tsa*), printed prayers, a ritual vase, mantras, and important relics. To create a stupa, permission must be received from spirits and earth deities. Auspicious vases are placed in the foundation at five points, and a centre pole of life is inserted in the middle. Proportions and shapes of the stupa vary but should follow the instructions in relevant sacred texts.

The huge dome of Bouddhanath stupa on the outskirts of Kathmandu is topped with a gilded square *harmika*. Painted on each of the four sides of the harmika are the all-knowing eyes of Vairochana, the Great Illuminator. Also known as the Supreme Buddha, the eyes symbolize awareness and cast a protective gaze across the Valley. During Losar, the festival of the Tibetan New Year, we Kathmandu residents gather together on the lower terraces of the stupa to throw *tsampa* (barley flour) and wish for good fortune and health. New strings of prayer flags are strung from the spire to below the dome, which is blessed with fresh arcs of saffron and mustard oil.

ABOVE:

In Ugyen Chholing, Bhutan, prayer wheels spin behind arches decorated with lotus and jewel motifs.

RIGHT:

Tsa-tsa, stupa-shaped clay votives made in moulds. They are offered at shrines and often placed by the thousands in the centre of stupas.

LEFT:

A stupa balanced upon a rock overlooks the valley by Samye Monastery, Tibet.

THE SPIRIT IN THE LANDSCAPE

Paths en route to monasteries and temples are marked by chortens or prayer walls bearing carved mani stones. These monuments in the landscape appear as a call to awareness as you cross fields and climb mountain trails. A pilgrim will circumambulate a chorten three times clockwise before continuing on his journey, often with the next wall or chorten already within sight. Chortens may pay homage to an important lama and contain his burnt remains. They are also built as offerings to the local deities of mountains and rivers.

Below Shey Palace in Ladakh is a wilderness of chortens. Although they seem as natural as the clouds in the sky and the layers of mountain peaks, they are also separate from what surrounds them. They are their own community and when the late sun of the day lights them you can't help but feel that they are thinking, pulsing, praying – in fact, the king had ordered prisoners to build these chortens as acts of merit. Their power stirs you as you stand dwarfed amongst them.

ABOVE:

A cluster of chortens in Ladakh. The tallest with its orange spire is topped with a crescent moon and a sun. The moon represents compassion and the sun wisdom and understanding.

OPPOSITE CLOCKWISE:

A Tibetan-style chorten, with a cylindrical top on a square base, lies on a crest above a wide valley, Drak Yerpa, Tibet.

Chortens once built by prisoners to attain merit are part of the landscape below Shey Palace, Ladakh.

Rectangular chortens topped by banners and containing prayer wheels in Thirthapuri, Tibet, near Mount Kailash.

Chortens and apricot blossoms along the roadside in Nurla village, Ladakh.

PRAYER FLAGS

Prayer flags become part of the natural landscape, complementing slopes and ridges. They may be consecrated by a lama before they are strung, branch to branch, cliff to cliff, in a high windy place. Looking to the sun through the multiple sheets of colour beating in the wind, one is moved by all the layers of faith, compassion and goodwill that they represent.

The flags are printed with mantras and prayers, which are spread by the wind to benefit all sentient beings. *Lung-ta* is the wind horse, an image often printed on prayer flags and representing good fortune. With the aid of the wind, the horse journeys across the sky to spread Buddhist teachings. Flags are blue (sky), white (air and wind), red (fire), green (water), and yellow (earth). As the colours fade with the elements, fresh ones are strung and blessings repeated.

Common in Bhutan are clusters of tall flag poles that are erected in windy places, such as ridges above river valleys. Some prayer flags billow on poles that stand strong and straight like sentinels, while others are tied to slim poles that lean in the wind. Traditionally, 108 poles with flags commemorated a death, the flags bearing prayers to Chenresig, the Bodhisattva of Compassion.

LEFT:

Monks and local villagers join in raising a flag pole in Tang Valley, Bhutan.

OPPOSITE CLOCKWISE:

Coloured flags flutter on a ridge above Trongsa Dzong, Bhutan.

Long flags wave from a cantilevered bridge near Tashi Yangtse, Bhutan.

Prayer flags along the kora at Drak Yerpa, Tibet. Ladders painted on the rock point the path to enlightenment.

A stupa at Ugyen Chholing with a view over the Tang Valley, Bhutan.

Prayer flags strung from trees at Nagi Gompa, Nepal.

Flags on tall poles in central Bhutan, commemorating a death and invoking compassion.

SACRED RITUALS AND OFFERINGS

In evoking the deities on earth, masked dances serve to establish harmony and balance amongst the many forces of the universe. Imbued with layers of meaning, they are an integral part of many Hindu and Buddhist festivals in the Himalayas. Life cycle rituals, and numerous other rituals throughout the year, are significant and often colourful events that require great care and preparation to please the gods.

The ritual ingredients arranged on a small leaf plate and offered to the deities contain a universe of meaning. Butter, cotton wicks, and kata (silk ceremonial scarves) are common offerings of Buddhists whereas Hindu peoples worship their deities with coloured powders and flowers. In Kathmandu, during the autumn festival season, markets abound with marigolds and a purple flower called *gwe swan*, a flower that doesn't wilt. It is offered on Bhai Tika, a day of honouring brothers.

In daily life the practice of making offerings is essential. Given with purpose and attention to images of deities – a Hibiscus flower placed behind a sculpted ear, a touch of powder on a gilded forehead – offerings are also transient. The deities in public shrines change their appearance continually as they receive powder and petals, coins and rice from their worshippers who visit them throughout the day.

Sacred places are found throughout rural and urban landscapes. A deity in the form of a rock protrudes from the cement of an urban street, the rising root of holy tree impedes the flow of traffic. Worship is not only tied to place: Hindu holy men journey through the Himalayas powerfully conveying their devotion with bold colour painted on their faces and bodies. Goats spotted with *tikka* powder or yaks and horses wearing ornaments and brightly woven saddles also carry vibrant messages to the gods.

CLOCKWISE:

In a window niche of Götz Hagmüller's home, a stone in a brass goblet becomes a lingam.

With Radha at his side, Krishna plays his flute in a shrine in Bhaktapur.

During the Maha Shivaratri festival in Pashupatinath, Nepal, a sadhu mixes *tikka* powder to apply to his body.

Two small brass donor figures stand in a Patan shrine.

Newar offerings during the ninth day of Dashain festival, Nepal.

A young man at the Brahmayani Temple in Bhaktapur sits for hours balancing oil lights to accrue merit for his family.

CLOCKWISE:

A masked dancer in the Mani festival in Humla. Marking the spring season, the dance brings supernatural forces down to the world of men.

Offerings made for Bartaman, the important rite of passage ceremony for boys. Dishes made of leaves hold grains, beans, and tikka powder.

Yogurt, an apple, and an egg are among the offerings on a silver tray prepared by a Newar worshipper.

During the festival of Dashain, ready-made leaf dishes are sold to hold offerings presented at temples. Offerings include marigolds, rice, lamp wicks, and red cloth.

CLOCKWISE:

Lakhbatti (100,000 wicks) are offered in thanks at the Baglamukhi Temple in Patan when one's wish has been fulfilled.

A Newar-Brahmin priest initiates a ceremony by putting tikka paste on a brass oil lamp.

Offerings are made with fresh flowers such as carnations and marigolds.

Marigold flower offerings are abundant during the autumn festival season.

An offering box carried by a worshipper during the ninth day of Dashain in Bhaktapur includes a pot of vermilion, wicks, rice, biscuits, coins, sugar, and flower petals.

CLOCKWISE:

The Buddha image worshipped with tikka powder and flowers, Swayambhunath, Kathmandu.

Lokeshwar, God of Compassion, Swayambhunath.

Amitabha Buddha, Swayambhunath.

An image of the goddess Brahmayani is worshipped at the Brahmayani Temple, Bhaktapur, on the ninth day of the festival of Dashain. The goddess is one of the nine forms of the goddess Durga, the Supreme goddess whose female power and energy (*shakti*) combines the energy of all the Hindu gods.

OPPOSITE CLOCKWISE:

The bowl held by a sculpture of Buddha, Swayambhunath, is filled with offerings of rice.

An offering made on the ground before a threshold in Bhaktapur.

An image of goddess Saraswati at the Maiti Devi Temple, Kathmandu.

Components of an offering include flower petals, tikka powder, rice, and beans.

CLOCKWISE:

In the Palanchowk Bhagwati Temple, Nepal, the ancient images of deities and a Shiva lingam emerge under layers of tikka powder.

A stone Shiva lingam is worshipped with a string of marigolds in Solu, Nepal.

The three yellow stripes on a lingam in Jumla, Nepal, represent the three-fold aspect of Shiva. As god of all gods, he fulfills the role of creating, preserving, and destroying.

OPPOSITE:

A Shiva lingam in Kirantishwar, Pashupatinath, Kathmandu. The lingam is the most holy object of Shiva worship. It represents the creative power of Shiva, as well as his power to transform sexual energy into spiritual energy. Natural rocks with the lingam form are especially sacred and become the focus of small shrines.

CLOCKWISE:

Offerings on a stone Shiva lingam in Patan.

A Shiva lingam at Pashupatinath, Nepal's most revered Hindu temple.

During the festival of Maha Shivaratri, Kathmandu, a Shivaite (follower of Shiva) sadhu paints *trishuls* (tridents) on his body.

An ancient temple in Hadigaun, Kathmandu, has been engulfed by a huge pipul tree.

OPPOSITE CLOCKWISE:

LEFT: A bell and shrine are sheltered within an ancient pipul tree by the Baglamukhi Temple, Patan.

In Hadigaon, Kathmandu, women offer cloth and string on a pipul tree in hope that they will be granted a son. The tree is considered female and therefore associated with fertility.

Dogs are worshipped on Kukur Tihar, the second day of the festival of Tihar in Nepal.

THE SPIRIT IN THE BUILDING

As we consider Himalayan styles, we must look at the whole process by which Himalayan peoples have settled and adapted to their challenging environment. Using local mud, stone, and timber they have created dwellings that withstand monsoon rains, harsh winds or snow. Yet they would consider no building to be durable if it were not somehow linked to a greater spiritual realm.

As the world today deals with issues ranging from environmental degradation to disintegration of community, it is timely to look at age-old patterns of construction in the Himalayas. The shelters and sanctuaries that we revere today – how were they constructed, and according to what aesthetic, communal, and spiritual principles? Himalayan 'style' has often been formed by geomantic, astrologic, and spiritual conceptions. When you are about to build a home in the Himalayas you cannot do so without first consulting an astrologer who tells you when to begin. The laying of the foundation stone requires a ceremony. More rituals accompany every step of the building process, which is concluded by the consecration ceremony. After moving in, you must be dutiful in performing rituals for your house deity: in this way your house is an entity that is as living as the people who dwell inside.

Within the earth beneath every building site is a vital force that you must reckon with, a notion reflected in a legend concerning the famous Jokhang Temple in Lhasa. The writhing movement of an ogress below the earth required the building of thirteen temples to pin her down, a process starting with the great Jokhang and including the Jampa Lhakhang in Bumthang, Bhutan.

If you are Tibetan and about to build your house, you make offerings to the earth deities with butter, tea, rice, and beer. You present white ceremonial scarves (kata) to the chief builders. Then when your house is completed, you hold a 'releasing celebration' to inaugurate your house and pay honour to the master builder. Similarly, if you are Bhutanese, you begin construction with a consciousness that your

building is not your own building, but belongs to a serpent spirit (*lu*) existing long before and after you. The lu resides in the ground and you will never see it. Yet you must remember during every step of construction that the land is not truly yours: your building is connected to the earth and to the spirit as well as to the community around you. Because the building of your house is disruptive to the harmony in the landscape, you must therefore appease the spirits, and only if you construct your house in this way can your house truly shelter you.

Each time you are adding a door, a balcony, or a roof you call the lamas who will conduct a ritual. As each pre-fabricated element is added to the building, the tip of a pine tree is tied to that place along with a kata. When the house is finished, it is time to hold the final *drub* ceremony. Perhaps you will string a short decorative curtain just below the roof, and hang large carved wooden penises at each of the four corners of the house to protect your house from evil. You will call seven monks to conduct rituals in which they blow horns and a shell and bang cymbals. Neighbours will join you to celebrate with song and food. Should your house later be thought to be overtaken by evil spirits (for instance, if someone falls ill or dies), you may need to abandon it forever. It is wise, therefore, to conduct an annual ritual for your house deity.

Today even modern cement structures are built with adherence to ritual: at the same time that local painters paint elaborate entablature under the eaves of a new cement hotel in Bhutan, a group of monks chant and blow horns inside – an important but noisy ceremony that will go on for a week. In the Himalayas a building is comprised of both spirit and matter – matter being the local materials worked by local craftsmen. But without attention to the spirit, the building is without firm and lasting foundation. Then, even when it is consecrated pr operly, you must remain cognizant of the spirits and deities that continue to govern your house.

PART 3
TRADITIONAL
LIVING
IN THE HIMALAYAS

In the high Himalayas people share common building materials, such as dressed or undressed stone with mud mortar, mud brick, and rammed earth. Walls are thick for the purpose of insulation and show the hand of man: there are few sharp corners or smooth surfaces. In the villages and towns, where people built structures that suited their environments, are examples of design that is both functional and aesthetic.

Construction is an event as much as a process, with a team that may be comprised of both men and women singing as they carry timber, build mud walls, or create floors. The flat roofs in Tibet are made of *arga* clay that is tamped down by teams of women who sing with gusto and step in rhythm, following a shared repertoire of songs and dances. Corners of the roof are decorated with bunches of branches and prayer flags that seem to suggest that the roof is bearing life. These branches and flags add colour and gaiety to the roofscape of a Tibetan village and send into the sky hopes of good fortune for all sentient beings.

Many daily activities occur on roof terraces, porches or courtyards: for families with animals and crops this is a utilitarian space where animals may be milked, fodder dried, and harvested grains processed. The ground floor of the house shelters animals and fodder, and the upper floors are used by the family. Interior furnishings are sparse, yet for the kitchen, the heart of the home, objects of lasting beauty are created. During free time a bowl may be carved, a basket woven. With their patina from so many years of smoke, butter, oil and touch, the objects – Bhutanese bamboo butter containers, Tibetan wooden spice boxes, Ladakhi ceramic vessels for chang – grow more beautiful with time. Their shapes and sizes are not uniform: seeing them displayed on a kitchen shelf you appreciate how each object has its own character.

The north-facing side of a three-storey stone house in Barkhang village, Humla, Nepal. The ground-floor shelters animals and contains a shrine for subduing subterranean spirits, the middle storey is used for cooking and sleeping, and the top storey, close to the gods, has the family altar. The roof is used for drying grains and vegetables such as buckwheat and radishes. It is layered with mud, flat stone, birch bark, and branches or boards. Stones are laid on the top along the perimetre. Using hand-carved wooden shovels, the residents frequently clear the roof of snow to prevent water damage.

BUILDING STYLES IN THE HIMALAYAS

In the mountainous regions of Tibet, Nepal and Ladakh, flat mud roofs are most practical. The roofs create another 'room' of the house, open to the air and sun, perfect for drying the foods and fodder that must last over a winter. In Nepal's middle hills you may still glimpse houses blanketed with thatch that from a distance looks soft and dense as fur, but most often thatch has been replaced with corrugated metal. Bhutan's houses have different variations of 'flying roofs' that allow for ventilation and for strong winds to pass straight through. They are traditionally topped with wood shingles that are weighted down with stones. Windows are shaped, carved and painted in styles distinctive to the region and are small to conserve heat.

OPPOSITE ABOVE:

Flat-roofed stone houses in Barkhang village, Humla, Nepal, have open terraces used for many activities, from winnowing grain to dancing during wedding ceremonies. At an elevation of 9,700 feet, the village looks out toward the fertile Nyin (sunshine) Valley.

OPPOSITE BELOW:

A stone farmhouse in Bhutan with raised roof covered with shingles, rabsel with white *ekra* panels, and porch reached by a ladder stair.

CLOCKWISE:

A tiny window set in a rough stone wall in Manang, Nepal.

Women tamp clay into the floor of a rammed earth house under construction in Bhutan.

Rows of small shuttered windows with an arched shape called *horzing* or *horzu* are common in Bhutan.

HAND-CRAFTED OBJECTS OF THE HOME

CLOCKWISE, OBJECTS FROM NEPAL:

A bronze water pot (*lota*) from the middle hills.

Turned wooden containers decorated with brass, used for keeping *rakshi,* or rice wine.

Hand-hewn wooden plates on top of a striped blanket from Dolpo.

A carefully carved handle (*neti* or *ghurra*) used for churning butter. A domestic folk art produced throughout Nepal's middle hills, these handles show the carver's creativity and skill. Birds, animals and plants provide inspiration for many ghurra designs.

OPPOSITE CLOCKWISE:

A well-worn door handle in Bhutan.

A wave pattern carved on a shutter in Bhaktapur, Nepal.

Brass ladles strung in a kitchen in Bhutan.

Detail of a wooden water container from eastern Tibet.

A measuring vessel (*mana*) from Nepal, stamped with the year 1945.

Endless knots and other auspicious Buddhist symbols carved on a wooden chest from Humla, Nepal.

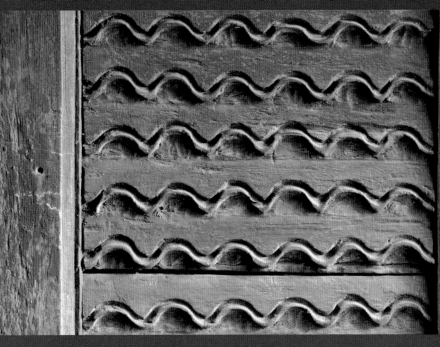

TRADITIONAL LIVING IN NEPAL

In a country with more than forty ethnic groups and a rich cultural history, styles of houses are many and reflect the character and resources of the local environment. We have chosen to focus on the styles of three distinctive regions, though were it possible we would embrace the entire diversity of Nepal's vernacular styles, including the simple stone, mud, and timber houses of the Gurung people and the bamboo houses of the Rai.

In Nepal's middle hills that slope to fertile valleys, farmhouses are often coloured with mud and clay or a lime wash and blend into the landscape. Villages may be clustered along ridges and hilltops, keeping fertile land available for agriculture.

The people who have settled above ten thousand feet in the district of Humla, a remote district in Nepal's far west, are Bhotia, or Tibetan-speaking people of Tibetan origin. The Bhotia practice fraternal polyandry (two or more brothers married to the same wife) and so their stone houses shelter many family members. Their folk Buddhism incorporates ancient shamanic practices and colourful festivals including a three-day masked drama (Mani) performed in the spring.

Houses in the district of Mustang, bordering Tibet, follow Tibetan style, with mud plaster covering flat-roofed buildings made of stone. Belief in Bon (pre-Buddhist) religion and Buddhism is evident in the strong stripes of earth colour on houses, monasteries, stupas, and prayer walls. The colours represent the Three Protectors (*rigsum gonpo*) who are ever-present both in settlements and along the trails that cut across the dry and mostly barren landscape.

Farmhouses along a ridgetop in Kavre district. They are coloured with local pigment. Roofs are covered with straw and tile and, more recently, corrugated metal.

A VILLAGE IN THE MIDDLE HILLS

Outside the Kathmandu Valley, where hills are dry red earth and most of the population is Buddhist Tamang, there lives a community of Newars. Their settlement, Saathighar (meaning 'sixty houses') was likely on an old trade route. As it is located off a main road, the village has changed little. The houses are maintained carefully by painting the old carved windows and applying fresh orange mud to the walls. Each year for the festival of Deepawali people make the house especially attractive for Laxmi, the goddess of wealth. Houses are cleaned and lights are lit, and a mood of cheer and rejuvenation permeates the village.

Those who travel from village to village, laden with a heavy basket or backpack, will stop under the shade of a *chautara*. The chautara is a rest place marked by a pipul and barra tree. The pipul is a sacred fig tree, also known as the bodhi tree that in Buddhism represents happiness and prosperity. The barra is a banyan tree, symbolizing everlasting life. Together they represent the male and female principles and add harmony to a village setting.

OPPOSITE CLOCKWISE:

An ancient chautara is preserved at the roadside.

Snakes, or *nagas*, are worshipped during the festival of Nag Panchami. To protect the house, colourful depictions of nagas are attached above the door.

The ground floor is often used for sheltering animals and storing fodder.

ABOVE:

Mud and rock walls are plastered with orange-coloured mud.

Newar carving can be seen in simplified form in second-storey window frames.

Bright blue paint is used on the wood elements of many of the village houses.

CLOCKWISE:

A house with the stucco features of Rana period style contrasts with its more recent neighbour in Gomsha, Kathmandu Valley.

In front of her farmhouse, a cheerful Nepalese woman poses with her goats.

Woven collapsible raincoats called *ghoom*, baskets for carrying fodder, and a straw mat are stored in front of a farmhouse in Lamjung district.

OPPOSITE CLOCKWISE:

A bamboo swing or *ping* erected in a village during the Dashain festival.

A three-storey brick farmhouse in Kavre district, with roof and balcony supported by wooden struts.

Thatch on a traditional mud-plastered farmhouse in Surya Binayek village.

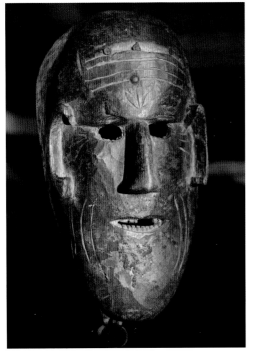

HUMLA

Along the Tibet border in northwestern Nepal, from where you can begin the journey to Mount Kailash, lies the remote district of Humla. Here the stone buildings of the Bhotia (Tibetan speaking peoples) are clustered tightly to save arable land. When you see the flat roof terraces connected by logs with carved steps, you can't help but think of the game of snakes and ladders. But life in Humla is demanding and the ladders attest to the agility of the inhabitants. These exterior ladders link multiple storeys, and are sometimes carved with an auspicious symbol at the top. On their flat roofs in the warm sun, people perform rituals, sew and weave, dry turnips, or thresh their barley and wheat.

RIGHT: Ladders made from single tree trunks lean from roof to roof in Kagalgaon village, and white prayer flags billow from long poles. Ladders may be carved at the top with Buddhist symbols such as the crescent moon and sun.

BELOW: The flat roofs of houses in Kagalgaon are used for a range of household and agricultural activities including the storage of firewood and hay.

OPPOSITE CLOCKWISE:

Stone houses of Brassi village, at an elevation of 11,770 feet, are clustered against the hillside with vegetable patches in between.

Masked dancers perform in the Mani festival held in the spring. They wear coats with stripes representing rainbows and belts with cowry shells, that were once used as currency. They dance to exorcize demons who harboured in the soil during the winter – so that fields will be fertile for spring.

An old dance mask from Humla depicts a lined human face.

MUSTANG

Once a medieval kingdom on the trade route between Nepal and Tibet, the region of Mustang stretches across a rugged high desert plateau. Here the earthy man-made structures reveal strong spiritual beliefs and are seemingly integral with the awe-inspiring, richly-coloured landscape of eroded mountains and dry plains.

Houses and chortens are striped vertically with contrasting natural earth colours. The shades of red, white and gray or blue represent three protectors of Tibetan Buddhism: Manjushri, Avalokisteshvara, and Vajrapani.

Called rigsum gonpo, these powerful gods protect the village against the malevolent spirits of the sky, earth, and netherworld. White is also the colour of the gods, red of the demons (*tsen*), and blue the serpant spirits (lu).

Colours of the protectors may change from village to village, depending on the locally available clay. Although the protectors are commonly represented as three chortens, their presence is also evoked through colour on the walls of houses and monasteries, as well as on trees and boulders.

PROTECTED PASSAGEWAYS

CLOCKWISE:

A passageway between connected buildings whose red-painted corners guard against demons (tsen).

A passageway to Samar village with a prayer wheel in the room above.

Male and female protectors at the entrance of Jharkot, a village in lower Mustang.

OPPOSITE:

The surrounding wall of a monumental building beneath the dramatic cliffs of Dhakmar is painted with the protective colours of the rigsum gonpo.

THE PROTECTED LANDSCAPE

RIGHT:

Protective stripes encircle the base of a chorten outside the village of Syangboche (3800 m) on the way to Ghiling village.

BELOW:

Stripes made with the pigments of local clay protect a corral in Samar village.

OPPOSITE:

Bold stripes evoke the three protectors on a boulder jutting above Chhunggar village.

ABOVE:

In the walled town of Lo Manthang houses are built close to each other and are accessible through narrow lanes and staircases. Firewood covers parapets, serving to protect the roof from rain or melting snow.

RIGHT:

Stripes of grey, orange and yellow, colours of the Three Protectors, are painted on walls of rammed earth or stone.

OPPOSITE CLOCKWISE:

Chortens and a mani wall at the eastern entrance of Tangye village.

A house entrance in Lo Manthang. Whitewashed walls are splashed and painted for protection.

Stripes and shadows on a rock wall outside Ghyakar village.

The firewood that is stored on roof parapets of Lo Manthang
protects the mud walls from rain and snow.

ROBERT POWELL: THE MUSTANG PAINTINGS

For many of us who live in the Himalayas, Robert Powell's paintings have changed the way we look at building structures, shrines, ritual objects, and other elements in our day-to-day life. How often we exclaim about a sacred tree or the textured wall of a Himalayan house: "That looks like a Robert Powell!" An architect by training, Powell has lived and worked in Asia for forty years. His work transcends the limitations of architectural drawing and documentation, incorporating his own often dream-like vision. Hence an eroded rammed-earth building from the high Himalayan settlement of Mustang becomes shaped like a sea-going vessel; the interior pillars of a Mustang temple, receiving light from a source above, seem to extend into infinity; and a house in Lo Manthang appears almost clownish with its striking black and red paint and a roof supporting curvy dried branches and twigs. Robert Powell identifies the unusual textures, materials, and colours in a man-made wall or edifice, highlights them and animates them. His art convinces us that we have never looked hard enough at our Himalayan environment, and once we study Robert's paintings, we see our surroundings anew.

TITLED FROM ABOVE:

The Eight Chortens of Lo.

Houses in Lo Manthang.

Rigsum gonpo, the Three Protectors, at
the Eastern Entrance to Tangye.

131

HOUSES OF LADAKH

The stories of a Ladakhi house represent the order of the cosmos: the lower floors with stables and storerooms correspond to the subterranean world of earth spirits (lu); the first floor represents the surface world with trees and rocks; and the top floor – where a prayer room facilitates communication with the gods – the sky. When you see a traditional home standing amidst poplars and willow trees, you notice how it fits peaceably with the surrounding landscape.

Ladakh, like other Himalayan regions, is undergoing rapid change. Traditional building methods and materials – stone, mud brick, and rammed earth with timber framing – are being substituted by cement. Tin roofs are replacing the flat mud roofs whose rims are distinctively piled with alfalfa for fodder in winter months. With so many traditional homes falling into decay, we were pleased to find a couple in Stok preserving a family house as a museum. Similarly, we met the descendants of two important ministers who are reviving the grand houses of their ancestors and turning them into guesthouses.

The ceilings and floors of the house of the Lhanpo (minister) in Alchi are caving in, but the example of the Munshi House in Leh (see Part 1) shows how such a ruin can be saved. The Nangso House in Nimmu, built by the king's interior minister and a large landholder, survived damage from Ladakh's devastating 2010 flood and will showcase unique features of traditional Ladakhi homes if it can be preserved. Here you see an altar room that can be closely circumambulated by way of an open terrace and balcony; a room for a visiting lama with attached altar room and toilet; a kitchen with fine copper pitchers for tea and chang; and a grain storage room with its *lubang*, or altar for the earth spirits who must be appeased.

The former house of the Alchi Lhanpo, a ruin that his heirs hope to restore, rises above the flat roofs of the village farmhouses. The structure on the hill above the Lhanpo's house, called a *lhato*, marks the presence of a local spirit.

THE LADAKHI VILLAGE HOUSE

CLOCKWISE:

An interior wall painting depicts a seated ruler and two rollicking snow lions.

Nearby farmhouses in Nimmu village are walled circular spaces where animals can thresh grain.

The worn steps between floors of a farmhouse.

OPPOSITE CLOCKWISE:

The Nangso house in Nimmu, once the home of a king's minister.

The kitchen of the Nangso house has a traditional ceramic stove, shelves of brass and copper pots, and a table built around a holy pillar.

A brass teapot with a silver dragon handle and *makara* spout.

A small screened room, influenced by Kashmiri style, is adjacent to a large room used for gatherings.

CLOCKWISE:

The traditional kitchen of the Gyabthawoo house, Stok village.

The grain storage room of the Nangso house, with its *lubang* (altar for the house spirit) in a corner by the window.

Wide-rimmed ceramic pots used for water in the Gyabthawoo kitchen.

OPPOSITE CLOCKWISE:

Animals graze within a mud-walled corral in Stok.

The impressive residence of the Alchi Lhanpo, awaiting restoration.

The altar room on the top of the Alchi Lhanpo's house.

Painted exterior of the altar room in Ama Tunu's house, Nurla.

A special suite (*zimchung*) in the Nangso house, which would be occupied by a high lama.

Entrance to the altar room adjacent to the zimchung of Nangso house.

AMA TUNU PRESERVES HER HOME

Most of the eight children she raised in the house have grown and left now, and her grandchildren are away at school. But Ama Tunu, age 74, maintains that while she is still alive her traditional house in Nurla village will be preserved.

Passing time in a traditional kitchen, enjoying tea or chang, is one of the special experiences for a visitor to Ladakh. In Ama Tunu's winter kitchen you sit on a Tibetan carpet and look up at shelves of copper and brass pots displayed in neat stacks and rows. The town of Chilling, first settled in the 16th century by Nepalese craftsmen, is noted for its production of beautiful pots, such as dragon-handled teapots and chang pots that are typically lined on a kitchen's top shelf. You learn that some of the pots have been with this household for generations, some have left with a daughter who has moved away, while others have recently come with a bride. Throughout time the pots will move this way between the houses of related families.

The hearth is sacred. In front of the stove of her kitchen are two pillars – one female, one male. Attached to the female pillar is a stand for an oil lamp, which is lit for the goddess of the hearth who resides behind Ama Tunu's stove. Ladakhi homes often have two different kitchens for warm and cold seasons. The larger of the two, the winter kitchen, is where the family can sleep and stay warm. The stove in the summer kitchen is made of clay with auspicious symbols depicted along its sides – craftsmen used to come to the house to make these stoves with a special kind of clay, but people don't want the clay stoves any more. Her winter kitchen has a stove made with steel sheet and decorated with brass and copper auspicious symbols that honour the spirit of the stove. The stove-maker is of the *garra* (blacksmith) caste. The garra use steel from Indian army drums to make stoves that blend the style of the traditional Ladakhi ceramic stove with the modern iron stove design brought to Ladakh by Moravian missionaries.

ABOVE:
Ama Tunu's rammed earth home in Nurla village.

RIGHT:

Pitchers, plates, and bowls are neatly displayed on kitchen shelves.

OPPOSITE CLOCKWISE:

Ama Tunu's summer kitchen has a clay stove, while the stove in her winter kitchen is a more modern style made by local blacksmiths (garra).

Photos and statue in the chapel on the top floor of the home.

Her winter stove is decorated with endless knot and jewel motifs.

INTERIOR FURNISHINGS OF TIBET

When you visit a Tibetan home, you sit on a painted bench topped by a colourful handwoven carpet. A teacup, removed from a storage cabinet decorated with floral motifs, is set before you on a low carved wooden tea table and will be filled again and again with hot butter tea.

The interiors of Tibetan homes across the vast region of Greater Tibet share a common aim: to create a happy and propitious atmosphere for family and guests. Wall decoration draws on a commonly shared Buddhist repertoire of symbols, and motifs that reflect good fortune. Furniture and carpets are also essential elements of these auspicious rooms.

It was in the monasteries that the Tibetan art of furniture-making likely developed. Items of furniture were created for many different functions: the high lamas needed tables when they sat upon their thrones; monks needed low tables when reciting prayers; outdoor ceremonies required folding tables; altar rooms needed tables for butter lamps and other offerings. Use of furniture become popular with the laity, whose commissions allowed painters opportunities for freer expression in their use of patterns, motifs, and colour.

While the development of Tibetan furniture was influenced by China, Mongolia, Central Asia and Nepal, it can be said that an aesthetic evolved that is truly Tibetan. Similarly, hand-woven carpets have a uniquely Tibetan identity. Given their tremendous variety in design, colour and detail, Tibetan furniture and carpets are considered by some experts to be Tibet's most expressive forms of traditional art.

The interior of Dolma Lhakhang in Spituk Monastery, Leh. The cabinet along the left wall contains 21 statues of Dolma (Tara) brought by the Dalai Lama from Tibet. The room exhibits elements of typical Tibetan style. A short curtain is painted on the wall below the ceiling and stripes of blue, red and green make a border on the wall and around the door. Brackets and cross beams are intensely painted. A couch for a high lama faces a finely carved table. Small painted chests and cupboards are used throughout the room.

FURNISHINGS FOR THE AUSPICIOUS HOUSEHOLD

CLOCKWISE:

Timber and rammed earth houses are set into the hillside in Gansi, Kham, Tibet.

Tea tables and carpets are arranged in the courtyard of Hemis Monastery, Ladakh, on the occasion of a feast.

A finely carved Tibetan table in a home in Bhaktapur, Nepal.

OPPOSITE CLOCKWISE:

Two pilgrims stand in front of the decorative bar of the Makya Ame restaurant located on the Barkhor (circumambulation area) in the old city of Lhasa.

Offerings at Losar, the Tibetan New Year celebration. Typical are large fried pastries called 'donkey's ears'.

In her home in Kham, a young woman sits on a painted bench softened by a carpet.

Detail of a table from Central Tibet, 18th–19th century. The decoration is elegant and is commonly known as 'red and black', an effect that is obtained when the gold leaf wears away and the remaining glue of the base oxidizes over the years and turns black creating a powerful contrast with the vivid red background.

ABOVE:

Gilded frames created in the workshop of Luca and Camilla Corona in Kathmandu employ the traditional raised gesso (*kyung bur*) technique.

OPPOSITE ABOVE:

Patterns of clouds, tiger stripes and the Chinese symbol for long life are painted on this cabinet from Kham, dating from the late 19th or early 20th century. The painting is bold and bright, rather like the Khampas themselves. Because of abundant timber in Kham, furniture tends to be more solidly built than the furniture in central Tibet where forests are scarce.

OPPOSITE BELOW:

Called a 'Lokha box' after the region in Tibet where it was made, this chest may date from the 15th century. The jewels of long life are depicted in the central cartouche. A tortoise shell pattern, seen in the detail on the far left, decorates the upper and lower panels.

ENDURING TRADITIONS

After studying for a Buddhist doctoral degree in a monastery in India, Italian Luca Corona travelled to Tibet where he was struck by the originality and variety of Tibetan furnishings. He then came to Kathmandu to set up a restoration workshop with an expert carpenter named Sega as his business partner. In addition to restoring pieces of old Tibetan furniture, their business also created new Tibetan-style crafts. Their range of mirror frames employs Tibetan techniques of gilding and raised gesso (*kyung bur*), two traditions that Luca knew from his home country.

Following the Cultural Revolution, a great deal of fine Tibetan furniture was carried out of Tibet into Nepal. The Tibetan carpet also travelled across the Himalayas and beyond. Here we pay special attention to saddle and sitting carpets in the collection of long-time Kathmandu resident Charles Gay. The snow lion remains an important symbol of Tibetan identity and its image continues to charm people around the world. Fortunately the Tibetan carpet-making tradition is still alive, though the majority of Tibetan-style carpet production is now located outside Tibet. The tradition has been invigorated through the work of designers such as Stephanie Odegard and Diki Ongmo whose carpets are highlighted in Chapter 5.

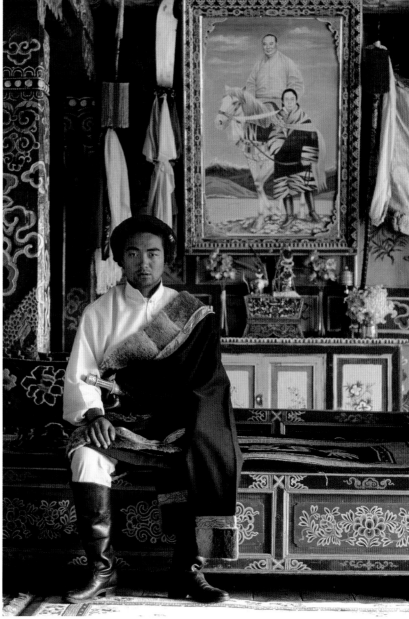

TIBETAN STYLE, OLD AND NEW

CLOCKWISE:

A Tibetan chest with carved panels in the home of Gert-Matthias Wegner, Bhaktapur.

A man from Kham poses in his family's house with colourful painted contemporary furniture.

In the Kelly home in Kathmandu an altar is created on a Tibetan cabinet.

OPPOSITE CLOCKWISE:

Following a traditional style that imitates a tiger skin, this contemporary tiger rug was produced in Lhasa using madder and walnut dyes.

In her carpet named 'Pema Tsetan shown in Cardamom' designer Stephanie Odegard reinterprets the traditional Tibetan lotus pattern.

The design of this contemporary carpet, produced by the Tanva workshop in Chusul, Tibet, is inspired by a Tibetan maze pattern.

A small chest is decorated with two snow lions on either side of flaming jewels.

AUSPICIOUS CARPETS

When Tibetan refugees first began arriving south of the Himalaya, carrying with them a variety of carpets woven for a wide range of uses, collectors and scholars were enchanted by the sophisticated Tibetan design sensibility. The snow lion was originally assumed to be an infrequent guest on Tibetan carpets, although it is considered the national animal of Tibet and appears on the Tibetan flag. In Tibetan legend, the snow lion represents boundless energy and fearlessness, based on purity of spirit, perfect wisdom, and compassion.

During the next few decades, as more carpets emerged from storage, it became evident that snow lions are actually represented reasonably often on saddle carpets, sitting carpets, and cushion carpets. The focus of my collection is on carpets that manifest this vast variety of snow lion motifs. Each of the present examples illustrates a unique Tibetan stylization, all have auspicious connotations, and in the Tibetan view, sitting on them brings good luck.

CHARLES GAY, on his collection

TOP: This saddle carpet was likely woven for a lama, as orange was usually reserved for the clergy. The anatomically awkward front facing smiling snow lions hold aloft wish-fulfilling jewels, offering them to the beholder. Ca. 1930s

ABOVE: Originally, a section of wool flat weave was sewn between the two halves of this carpet, fitting the carpet to the rider and the horse. This carpet shape, often called 'butterfly', usually dates from after the Younghusband expedition of 1904, the assumption being that the Tibetans were inspired by the shape of British saddle pads.

CLOCKWISE:

A relatively recent small sitting carpet features a jewel-bearing snow lion exuberantly bursting from its blue ground.

A small cushion carpet, notable for the snow lion's red mane and tail. Typically these features are green or blue, but in this example the ground colour itself is a vegetable dye blue-green. Ca. 1930s

The upper carpet of a saddle set. This same design, with this particular snow lion posture and expression, with a jewel inner border and a dragon and phoenix outer border, can be found in at least two other collections, with only minor variations, suggesting an origin in the same workshop, if not from the same weaver. Ca. 1930s

This unique small sitting carpet appears to have been highly venerated, as it has been expertly repaired several times. The snow lion presents a rather endearing lifelike expression, and the empty red background is rare. Early 20th century

THE FARMHOUSE AND PALACE IN BHUTAN

Having an easier climate and plentiful forest cover, Bhutan's architecture utilizes more wood and painted exterior decoration than its northern neighbour, Tibet. Houses are solidly built on stone foundations and the thick ground-storey walls are made of rammed earth or rough stone masonry. Sometimes projecting rows of windows (rabsels) are built on upper stories. Today, exterior walls are often whitewashed and bear lively images of snow lions, tigers, the garuda, and large phalluses, a protective symbol most common in rural areas.

Elegant and practical are the sloping roofs traditionally covered with spruce shingles. Typically a house has a central roof that overhangs one or two lower roofs. A gap between the roof and top floor allows air to circulate and keep stored grain dry. On top of the rooftops you often see patches of bright chilies drying in the sun.

The 19th century homes of Bhutan's aristocracy share a unique style. The power of the elite was represented by the complexity of exterior wooden and painted elements. Wide two-tiered rabsels, with carved and painted brackets underneath, covered most of the first- and second-floor storeys. Doorways were carved with the *pema-chudzo* motif, a feature traditionally reserved only for religious and aristocratic residences.

Below their eaves, aristocratic residences were allowed two rows of *boo*, square end beams that are painted with mantras. The space in between boo are called *ka,* which are painted with floral motifs. The row of upturned wood elements above the boo and ka are known as 'crane's neck' or 'pig's nose'.

The utse of Wangdichholing, Bumthang with its two tiers of wide rabsels. Shutters retain some of their original colour. Just under the roof one can see traditional timber elements called 'crane's neck' and two rows of decorative end beams, called boo.

RURAL STYLE

CLOCKWISE:

Walls of an old farmhouse slope inwards. Shingle roofs are weighted down by stones.

A farmer with his ox in the Tang Valley.

The upper storey of a small farmhouse near Trongsa has timber-framed windows with white painted wattle and daub or ekra panels.

Exuberant lotuses, auspicious symbols, flank a farmhouse doorway.

OPPOSITE CLOCKWISE:

Phallus symbols are painted on the walls of houses to ward away evil.

Bamboo fences line the pathway to a farmhouse near Bumthang.

A woven bamboo enclosure lies below the small house of a local spirit.

Small sacred buildings hold water-driven prayer wheels, Tang Valley.

HOMES OF KINGS AND NOBLES

19th century palaces of Bhutan's aristocracy are comprised of a large residential structure that encircles a courtyard and a main tower building (utse). The homes of lesser aristocrats are not as grand but, like palace structures, have sophisticated timber elements such as large two-tiered rabsels. Three examples of palace architecture are featured in the next pages. The impressive Wangdichholing Palace in Bumthang is temporarily a residence for monks, its future use yet to be determined. The Gangtey Palace in Paro, once the residence of the Paro Penlop, has been converted by his descendants into a hotel. Ugyen Chholing, an aristocrat's estate in Tang Valley, is now a museum that evokes a colourful past.

A house belonging to a royal relative (pictured right) near Jakar Dzong. Its wide two-tiered rabsels are typical of aristocratic buildings. It has a *jamthog* roof, or raised gable roof over a second roof structure.

WANGDICHHOLING

A visitor to Wangdichholing is surprised to learn that not long ago it was a seat of government: the weathered building is on its way to becoming a ruin. Monks occupy some of the upper rooms and the young monks can be heard reciting prayers. Still beautiful to behold, Wangdichholing contrasts remarkably with its crisp and clean modern neighbour, the Amankora Bumthang.

Wangdichholing, built in 1857, later became the main residence of the first king, Ugyen Wangchuk. It was used by Jigme Wangchuk, the second king, as a summer residence and until 1952 by the third Bhutanese king, Jigme Dorji. Once every window frame, door, balcony, and stairway was brightly painted. While small motifs decorated most timber elements, the wooden shutters of the rabsels were painted different solid colours (lapis blue, turquoise, red, or yellow) in an order that is not apparent. It is no wonder that these multicoloured rabsels with their carved brackets are considered the 'jewels' of a Bhutanese building. Yet it is hard to imagine how the palace once appeared when newly painted, the colours vivid. When the palace is one day renovated to serve a new function, its patina should be valued and preserved.

ABOVE: A brightly painted rabsel faces the interior courtyard. At the entrance are tapered columns (*kachen*) with decorative brackets *(zhu)*.

BELOW: Timber elements are painted with motifs such as jewels and lotuses.

155

ABOVE:

The exquisitely painted chapel room is on the top floor of the central utse. Its entrance is marked by colourful silk hangings. The wooden floor is left bare, except for a runner with a carpet where one can make prostrations.

LEFT FROM TOP:

The orange doors to the family shrine room (choesham) are carved with auspicious Buddhist symbols. Ancestral photographs are placed on the altar. The niches in the wooden altar display the family's fine collection of clay statues.

OPPOSITE:

The interior courtyard of Gangtey Palace, with exterior stairways linking levels. Typical of palace construction, an outer building encircles the central utse. In 1928, the utse was the residence of the King of Bhutan when he came to Paro.

A metal latch fashioned as a dorje.

GANGTEY PALACE

Built over one hundred years ago by the uncle of Bhutan's first king, the Gangtey Palace is today a hotel. Fortunately its owner, the grandson of Bhutan's first prime minister, has kept many of the original features intact – most notably the shrine room. The charming shrine room (*choesham*) on the utse's top floor is entered through bright orange lhakhang doors that are carved with auspicious Buddhist symbols. The walls are fully painted with religious deities and other Buddhist imagery, and katas are draped across the altar and wrapped around statues. The upper part of the altar displays ritual objects and statues, while the lower part contains prayer books, rolled thangkas, and other items not in daily use. At the altar the family makes daily offerings, filling brass bowls with water and ceramic vases with fresh branches of rhododendron blossoms.

ABOVE:

The *nay dom*, or sleeping box, was used both for sitting and meditation.

LEFT, FROM TOP:

The estate's two-storey temple building contains four lhakhangs used by the family and local villagers.

The water spirit, or lu, is depicted on a shrine building in the Ugyen Chholing courtyard. The lu, to whom the ground belongs, must be appeased regularly.

The four-storey main building (utse) is now a museum that recreates the living style of the religious nobility in the 19th–20th centuries.

The seat and writing desk of the family patriarch, with a brass betel box and spittoon placed nearby. Thangka paintings mounted on brocade hang above.

A traditional staircase with wooden pole railings leads up to a lhakhang in the temple building.

Silk banners mark sacred space in front of the family altar. The small niches hold statues. Offering bowls and pitchers for holy water are placed below.

UGYEN CHHOLING

When you are awakened in the new guesthouse on the estate premises by a farmer's shout to scare the boars from his field, you try to imagine how days at Ugyen Chholing used to have begun. Who rose first? What were the day's first sounds of activity? Women cooking the first meal of the day; trade merchants arriving tired and hungry from afar; resident monks tending the estate's lhakhangs; the inhabitants of surrounding farmhouses rising to labour in the fields?

The compound includes immense oak trees, a four-storey utse, a two-storey temple, and a surrounding residential building. Originally built in the 16th century and then reconstructed after an 1897 earthquake, the lovely Ugyen Chholing is now a museum. In its heydey, painted in bold hues of blue and reds, the estate would have reflected the esteem of its owners who are the descendants of the Saint Dorje Lingpa (1365-1405), an important *terton,* or discoverer of religious treasures. These descendants were called *Lama Choeje,* or religious nobility, and

they bore the responsibility of perpetuating religious traditions. The estate's lhakhangs were attended by monks who performed rituals for both the family and local villagers.

While it was most importantly a centre of spiritual activity, Ugyen Chholing was also the village hub for business and trade. Guiding the affairs of Ugyen Chholing from his administration room, the prestigious head of the estate used to send out his own merchants on trade missions to Tibet and India. From Tibet, the estate received gold dust, tea, cloth, and salt, and in turn traded cloth, leather, tobacco, paper, rice, sandalwood, and the natural dyes, indigo and madder.

Meanwhile, in rooms by the entry gate, talented women weavers from the local village were employed to weave exclusively for the estate. Cloth was an important asset of all households, and wealthy households produced the textiles Bhutan is famous for today. These textiles would increase in value over the years and constitute family heirlooms.

Panels of a kira, women's traditional dress, specially woven for the coronation of Bhutan's fifth king.

Aum Karma in front of traditional cloth woven in her weaving workshop near Thimpu.

KARMA YUNGCHEN: MASTER WEAVER AND INNOVATOR

In the past, royal and aristocratic families of Bhutan maintained workshops of weavers to weave their valuable cloth. Most of this cloth was woven for a woman's *kira* (wrap dress) or man's *gho* (a robe worn knee-length). Cloth is still woven today on a back-strap loom, and when woven in silk with numerous intricate patterns and motifs, it is one of the world's most unique and valuable textiles.

In 2009, in a small wooden structure on the side of Karma Yungchen's house, five master weavers wove royal ghos and kiras for the grand ceremony of the fifth king's coronation. While Aum Karma oversaw the completion of these robes, she was also chosen to weave cloth for new Druk Airlines uniforms. During this busy time she continued to innovate: her contemporary, naturally-dyed shawl won a UNESCO Award of Excellence and was exhibited in the Santa Fe International Folk Art Market. She also attended a natural dye workshop in Bangladesh and so now one will often find her making dye experiments in a shed behind her house. Banana flowers, peach leaves, and other plants she grows in her garden are found in her bubbling pots, while skeins of silk in soft hues hang on poles criss-crossing her drying room. Aum Karma is a soft-spoken woman who is at all times restless to experiment and create. Her traditional weavings are unsurpassed, while her innovations are bringing fresh air to Bhutan's famous weaving traditions.

A weaver in Aum Karma's workshop uses the supplementary weft technique to make intricate motifs.

Silk cloth woven for a gho, the traditional robe worn by Bhutanese men.

PART 4

HIMALAYAN RETREATS AND TRAILS

The Himalayas have long offered shelter for monks, pilgrims, traders, artisans, and other weary travellers. But with the development of trekking tourism, a new type of Himalayan retreat has emerged for those who wish an alternative to a simple bed by the hearth, tsampa, and butter tea. But although they may offer internet and cabernet, the retreats presented here nevertheless preserve Himalayan aesthetics and offer easy access to Himalayan culture, monuments, and nature.

In the next pages we visit the Amankora lodges, which are located in the proximity of a number of Bhutan's unique cultural sites, such as the Gangtey Gompa in Phobjikha Valley. The Hotel del Sherpa is located not far from the revered Chiwong Monastery in Nepal's Solu Khumbu district, homeland of the Sherpa people. In the Tibetan town of Gyalthang in China's Yunnan province, old rammed earth buildings have been carefully restored and converted into cafés and lodges. In India's Kumaon region, 360 Leti offers guests a mountain experience in simple but elegant guest houses built with local expertise and materials.

Three chortens representing the rigsum gonpo, the Three Protectors, on a ridge in Mustang, Nepal.

BHUTAN: THE AMANKORA LODGES

The traveller to Bhutan is likely to plan a journey that includes visits to Bhutan's famous dzongs and temples. As these structures are located in towns across the country, one crosses some distance on forested roads or foot trails before reaching the next spectacular site. The Amankora lodges are located in several favourite destinations such as Phobjikha Valley which contains Gangtey Gompa, an impressive monastery complex built on a hilltop. Amankora Punakha is not far from the splendid Punakha Dzong with its dramatic location at the confluence of the Mo and Pho rivers, and Amankora Bumthang directly faces the Wangdichholing Palace.

The architectural style of these retreats is inspired by the Bhutanese rammed earth buildings in surrounding villages. Design of the lodges incorporates traditional shapes and materials but is without the ornamentation that is locally popular today. Modest in scale, the lodges are set subtly into the landscape in order to provide both privacy and tremendous views.

CLOCKWISE:

The minimal style of the window panels of the Amankora Paro mirror the projecting windows (rabsels) of traditional houses. Windows give a view over an outdoor terrace and to Drugyal Dzong beyond.

Entrance to the Amankora Paro.

A detail from a building in the Gangtey Gompa complex.

View towards the dining room windows of the Amankora Bumthang. The structure with white slanted walls on the left houses guests.

A traditional farmhouse with rabsel in Paro.

Chortens and prayer flags border a stream in Paro Valley.

'Aman' means peace, and 'kora' is spiritual circumambulation. When you journey from one Amankora lodge to the next you will notice semblance in the design, which is meant to provide reassurance in an unknown land. At the same time, you are struck by features in each lodge that are a response to the local environment and unique cultural sites nearby.

The mud walls of the resort in Paro evoke the decaying mud walls of Drugyal Dzong, a dramatic ruin nearby. The name means 'fortress of the Victorious Drukpa', but in 1951 a fire turned Drugyal Dzong into a ruin that continues to look out over Paro Valley. Architect Kerry Hill has quoted an old Chinese proverb "the future is only the past again, entered through another gate". The design of these exclusive resorts returns to the fundamentals of traditional Bhutanese architecture, without today's popular overlay of decorative painting.

On a site facing the Wangdichholing Palace in Bumthang, Hill has designed a stark stone building that seems a considered response to the colourfully painted woodwork of the palace. With slanting white walls,

stacked timber-framed windows and no exterior decoration, the building maintains an earnest contemporary presence as it faces the ageing palace. The building complex includes a wide furnished stone terrace where visitors can enjoy a view of the palace and the hills beyond. This terrace, complete with fireplace, allows the visitor ample exposure to the scenery and open air while also providing all the protection and comfort of an indoor environment. On the other side of the main building is a unique stone walkway that links guestrooms, solemn as a long corridor in a dzong.

The rammed earth walls of the Amankora in Phobjikha Valley mirror those of the Gangtey Sang Nha Choling Monastery (Gangtey Gompa) nearby, before the monastery underwent repainting. The monastery has never been destroyed by earthquake or fire and so represents a truly historic building in its proportions and style. The recent renovation embellishes the historic structure in ways that match Bhutanese modern taste. We were able to photograph the renovation of

the monastery in process, while its walls were still a natural mud colour and the wood detail unpainted. The beauty of these unpainted elements is otherwise transitory. Most often only very old Bhutanese houses have unpainted walls – today they are plastered and painted, and timber elements much embellished with painted decoration.

To make the sloping rammed earth walls of the Amankora lodges, the mud was mixed with a small amount of cement and waterproofing agent. A metal framework was used for compacting the mixture, with the holes of tie-rods left in the walls, the same holes that are visible in traditional rammed-earth Bhutanese buildings before they are plastered.

The interior wood floors, walls and ceilings of the lodges reflect the simple use of timber in Bhutanese homes. Colours of upholstery are subdued, the wood furnishings are light in colour, and rooms are highlighted with Bhutanese objects or textiles, such as a naturally dyed nettle runner that decorates a bed, or a Bhutanese bowl that decorates a plain tabletop. Interior architect Albano Daminato designed unobtrusive

light fittings, special bukhari wood stoves, and round tables that repeat the forms of local bamboo containers for cheese and butter. Each room has a large bathroom that contains a wooden bath. The bathtubs are based on traditional Bhutanese wooden bathtubs that are placed outdoors. Hot rocks placed into the tub help heat the cold fresh water.

ABOVE:

View of the upper Paro Valley from the Amankora Paro.

OPPOSITE:

The rammed earth buildings of the Amankora Paro.

TOP:

Gangtey Gompa (monastery) as seen from Amankora Gangtey.

ABOVE:

The restored Gangtey Gompa with timber elements as yet unpainted.

RIGHT:

The interior corridor of Amankora Gangtey with stone paving, rammed earth walls, and timber ceiling.

OPPOSITE CLOCKWISE:

Natural materials are used in the rooms' interiors. Panelling reflects the wooden walls of Bhutanese houses.

Rear view of a building at Amankora Gangtey. Stairways are made with local stone. The roof structure is open, following traditional style. The plain wooden balcony is a minimalist version of a Bhutanese rabsel with ekra panels.

Amankora Gangtey whose arched timber window frames and slanted rammed earth walls reference local style.

CLOCKWISE:

A table designed by Albano Daminato (who was inspired by the shapes of Bhutanese containers) displays a Bhutanese turned wood bowl.

At the Amankora Gangtey a projecting wall of glass windows is a modern interpretation of the Bhutanese rabsel.

The paved corridor linking separate guest quarters at Amankora Bumthang has stone walls and a light timber ceiling.

The wall along a staircase at Amankora Paro resembles a typical Bhutanese dry-stacked stone wall.

The bathtub is modelled after a traditional hot stone bath.

Rammed earth buildings of Amankora Paro are clustered amidst pines like a small village.

SOLU KHUMBU: HOTEL DEL SHERPA

The mountainous district of Solu Khumbu is home to communities of Sherpa people who migrated there hundreds of years ago from Tibet. Manifesting their strong Buddhist beliefs, the landscape is marked by chortens, prayer flags, and mani walls. For local people and for followers from far away, the Tibetan Buddhist temples and monasteries established in Solu Khumbu are important centres for ritual and worship.

In building their own houses as well as lodges for tourists, Sherpas have utilized traditional materials and building methods. To protect against the monsoon rainfall, roofs in Solu are ridged and made of slate. Houses are elongated in shape and two-storey, with large front windows facing the valley. Brightly painted window frames and doors contrast walls built with roughly dressed stone. Within the house is an altar room, a private place of worship that is richly decorated with Buddhist imagery. The house of Ang Babu Sherpa, great grandson of Sangye Lama (the revered founder of Chiwong Monastery) exemplifies the local aesthetic in both its sturdiness and cheerful detail.

Located next door to Ang Babu's house is the famous Hotel del Sherpa, which also exhibits the traditional architectural features of Solu Khumbu and has delighted travellers for decades. Visitors to the hotel often make their way to Chiwong Monastery, where the great Nyingmapa Tibetan Buddhist festival of Mani Rimdu is held each year. Until recently it was graced by His Holiness Trulshig Rinpoche, founder of Solu Khumbu's Thupten Chöling Monastery where he presided over 900 monks and nuns.

CLOCKWISE:

Butter lamps on a tray at Chiwong Monastery.

Ritual bowl and spoon on a table covered with bright brocade.

An auspicious conch shell bracelet worn by a Sherpa woman attending the Mani Rimdu festival.

On special occasions a Sherpa woman wears a valuable silver repoussé clasp over the front of her woven waist wrap.

Cymbals used during the Mani Rimdu festival.

Monks at Chiwong monastery watch a performance of Cham dances. The monastery was built in the early 1980s by Sangye Lama who invited carpenters, masons, and painters from Tibet to share their skills with local Sherpa artisans.

It is early November when we approach the Hotel del Sherpa, climbing its neatly paved entryway that contrasts with the worn paths and walls of mani stones that feature in this mountainous terrain. Having flown in early on a helicopter from Kathmandu, we are happy to be served tea in the sun in the hotel's lawn chairs that afford a remarkable mountain view. But we cannot relax long, for it is a one and a half hour walk to the Chiwong Monastery. The Mani Rimdu celebration with its masked Cham dances takes place at the monastery each autumn in the 10th month of the Tibetan lunar calendar. Each year as we watch the dances and then receive blessings from the Rinpoche, we feel renewed.

The trail to the monastery grows colourful with local people dressed specially for today's ceremony. Women wear chubas, striped aprons

(*pangden*) with enormous silver clasps, and their best jewellery. The crowd buzzes as people find viewing space around the monastery courtyard; children's faces press against the rails of the crowded second-floor balconies. The deep notes of the *dung chen*, long Tibetan horns, further stir excitement. Over the hours, the monks dance to dispel demons and celebrate Buddhism's introduction to Tibet; at the end of the festival we are assured a year of peace and well-being. We arrive back late at the Hotel del Sherpa and are welcomed with wine and a hot dinner served from shiny brass vessels. Then we find our beds so that we may wake just as the first light touches the world's highest mountains.

OPPOSITE CLOCKWISE:

The shelves in Ang Babu Sherpa's kitchen display *momo* (dumpling) steamers, wooden vessels for *chang* (beer made from millet or barley), pitchers for rice wine, and pots for water.

A row of butter lamps below prayer books in Chiwong Monastery.

Primordial Buddha, Kuntung Zangpo, in *yab-yam* embrace on a ceiling painting in the chapel of Ang Babu's house.

ABOVE:

Along the path to Chiwong Monastery are prayer walls with mani stones covered with moss and ferns. Mani stones are inscribed with mantras or devotional images and are often placed in mounds or along walls often as offerings to the spirits of the place.

The well-equipped kitchens of Sherpa houses of the Everest region reflect Sherpa hospitality as well as great pride in the home. Wooden shelves and cabinets line the kitchen walls and neatly display brass plates, copper kettles, momo steamers, and brass and wood vessels. Large copper pots decorated with brass are used for storing water, and brass ladles are important daily implements. A household's bounty of cookware and serving vessels indicates its affluence. At Losar, the festival of the New Year, tsampa is dabbed on the smoke-darkened kitchen woodwork or used to draw auspicious symbols, ensuring prosperity and good fortune for the year to follow.

In the kitchen of Solo Khumbu's Hotel del Sherpa, Phu Lhamo and her team of cooks prepare delicious local cuisine such as momos, *dido* (millet paste that is dunked in soup), and a mushroom sauce made with local morels. The hotel was the creation of a leading Sherpa family in collaboration with Italian Count Guido Monzino, who led the first Italian expedition to Mount Everest in 1973. The dining room blends European opulence with the rich interior décor of a Buddhist temple. The walls bear images of the guardian kings, pillars and beams are painted brightly, and bottles of wine are kept within the niches of a colourful shrine cabinet-cum-bar. For decades, this room has surprised travellers who never expected to find such a hotel in the heart of Solo Khumbu District. The great explorers and climbers of the Everest region have stayed here, including Sir Edmond Hillary. In the spring when the rhododendrons are in bloom in the surrounding hills, and in the autumn during the Mani Rimdu festival at nearby Chiwong Monastery, it is here that we have been hosted as guests of Christopher Giercke, who has taken over care of the hotel for the owner, Jamling Sherpa.

OPPOSITE CLOCKWISE:

A Sherpa kitchen with its neatly arranged pots and utensils. Barley flour designs on the smoke-darkened wall bring good fortune at New Year.

Ang Babu's house, a traditional Sherpa house built by Sangye Lama, next to the Hotel del Sherpa.

Rows of shelves with pots and ladles in the kitchen of Thupten Chöling Monastery.

ABOVE:

In the painted dining room of Hotel del Sherpa, the table is set with brass dinnerware and silver cups.

CLOCKWISE:

Dragon image in a wall painting at Chiwong Monastery.

Children view *cham* dances from a decorated balcony.

On the panels of a monastery door, playful and feisty snow lions hold jewels of life.

The skeleton figure in the cham dance is the protector of the charnel ground who reminds onlookers of the transitory nature of existence.

Dragon and cloud motifs decorate a monastery door frame.

OPPOSITE CLOCKWISE:

The altar at Ang Babu's house next to the Hotel del Sherpa.

Snow lions are painted on end beams above the monastery entrance.

The late Honourable Trulsig Rinpoche, founder of Solu Khumbu's Thupten Chöling Monastery.

GYALTHANG: ALONG THE OLD TEA AND HORSE CARAVAN TRAIL

Known today as the 'Tea and Horse Caravan Trail', this more than one thousand year-old route comprises numerous, often treacherous trails connecting China, Tibet, India, and Burma. Not only tea and horses, but salt, jewellery and other items were traded along this complex and difficult route. In the period of the Tang Dynasty (618-907 AD) tea from Yunnan became an essential feature of Tibetan culture: in 1651 it was estimated that 1.5 million kilograms of tea from Yunnan were transported to Tibet. The most favoured type of tea was Pu'er tea from Pu'er Prefecture in southern Yunnan. The Tibetans developed their own way to drink this fermented tea – mixing it with butter and salt – and today butter tea remains a staple of the Tibetan diet with proven benefits to health.

Caravans heavily laden with tea departed from the Tibetan town of Gyalthang for a trip to Lhasa that would cover 1,000 miles over a period of months. Today one can still meet a few elderly traders who with nostalgia recall their arduous journeys up and down high mountain passes. The old trading town is now only a diminishing corner of a sprawling Chinese city, yet fortunately some of the old rammed earth homes and stone-paved streets remain intact, reminders of a fascinating era.

CLOCKWISE:

Racks for drying barley stand in the fertile fields.

A paved walking street in Gyalthang, an ancient town on the 'Tea and Horse Caravan Trail'.

Prayer flags printed with wind horses hang in front of a mud-plastered monastery wall.

THE RAMMED EARTH HOUSES OF GYALTHANG

Although they are now adapted with contemporary features such as warm 'greenhouse' rooms, houses in Gyalthang and surrounding valleys are still built with rammed earth and have finely carved timber elements on the southern façade and interiors. A central living and dining space is intended to be large enough to accommodate lively Tibetan wedding parties, and here the walls bear smoke-darkened paintings of the Tibetan auspicious symbols. In the nearby fields are tall racks for drying barley. The racks stand empty much of the year, then in autumn appear to bear great golden wafers, so densely packed is the grain.

Within the fast-changing town of Gyalthang are restoration efforts by residents, many who have settled there from other places, including Taiwan, Britain, France, Canada, the United States, Beijing, India, Lhasa, and Szechuan Province. They have endeavoured to preserve Gyalthang's historic architecture and have transformed a number of rammed earth and timber buildings into comfortable cafés, lodges, and private homes.

CLOCKWISE:

Rammed earth farmhouses near Gyalthang. Auspicious Buddhist symbols are painted under the eaves.

At Ringa Monastery prayer flags are printed with earth pigments.

Bunches of grain hang on a rack to dry.

Light-coloured mud plaster covers rammed earth walls.

In Gyalthang, a town along the old 'Tea and Horse Caravan Trail', streets are paved with stone.

Construction of new buildings follows tradition. Massive pillars are used in the frame and walls are built with rammed earth.

THE TARA CAFÉ

Uttara Sarkar Crees has made her own long journey to Gyalthang, once the rest-stop for traders in tea. Born in Uganda of Indian descent, Uttara came to Gyalthang via Kathmandu (her home of many years), and then began to restore some of the last remaining wood and rammed earth Tibetan houses in the historic old town. That Uttara herself is a Himalayan treasure is apparent when you hear her speak knowledgeably (in English, Tibetan, Chinese, Nepali, or Hindi) of this unusual place – its architecture or wildflowers, its past or future. She has dedicated much of her energy to environmental conservation and to efforts to preserve Gyalthang, which in recent years was renamed Shangri-la (after the fictional Eden in James Hilton's novel *Lost Horizon*).

Along a stone paved road that is part of the 'Old Tea and Horse Caravan Trail' is a tea merchant's house that is now the Tara Café. One of its 200-year-old rammed earth walls is carefully preserved and the aged timber elements are stained dark and varnished so that they glow warmly. On the lower floor, the room in which the tea merchant conducted his business transactions is now converted into a lounge; the walls, however, still contain secret compartments where he hid his valuables. The upstairs is converted into a cozy dining area and includes a small side room once belonging to a concubine of legendary beauty.

On cold winter nights in the café's living room we quickly warm up by the Canadian-made wood stove with a bowl of *thukpa* (Tibetan noodle soup) prepared by the head cook, Yampi. Among favourite items at Tara Café are the light *puri* served with a delicate eggplant mousse, and for dessert, a barley flour and walnut cake topped with local yogurt.

CLOCKWISE:

A 200-year-old tea merchant's house is now the Tara Café.

The chamber once reserved for the tea merchant's concubine is now a private dining area.

A wooden cabinet in the tea trading room holds wine and books.

Leading to a quiet dining area is a door carved with the symbol of happiness.

KARMA CAFÉ

On the terrace of the Karma Café, you have a full view over the shingle roofs of houses in Gyalthang's old town to a giant golden prayer wheel built in recent years on a small hill with a temple. Further in the distance are the softly curving mountains that circle the valley, still not quite touched by the burgeoning growth of Gyalthang's 'new town'. At Karma Café we dine on yak bourguignon served by Afang, an interior designer who opened the café in 2006. Afang is also one of the old town's protectors, having restored and tended with equal sensitivity two traditional rammed earth homes – one that houses the café and one where she and her two beloved Tibetan mastiffs reside.

The main room of the café is traditional to the Tibetan houses of this region: auspicious symbols are painted on panels of the walls that face a central stove, and the room contains two altars – one for the family and one for the water god. An immense holy pillar with traditional carved brackets stands at the centre of the room, a silk kata tied around it. Afang has added to the room a large appliquéd thangka made by monks she knows in Qinghai and depicting one of the great teachers of Tibetan Buddhism, Je Tsongkhapa.

Many winter evenings have been spent around Afang's wood-fired stove listening to stories of her journeys. Though often travelling through other Tibetan areas of China or back to her native Taiwan, Afang loves to return to this 200-year-old house which she claims has 'true spirit and soul'.

CLOCKWISE:

Auspicious symbols decorate one wall of the living room. Light filters down from an opening in the ceiling above a central hearth.

The guestroom door is covered by an appliquéd Tibetan curtain. Exterior wooden elements of Gyalthang houses are typically carved or painted with Buddhist symbols.

Copper kettles are made locally by people of the Bei minority.

A wooden altar to the water god contains a large copper water basin and brass ladles.

HOME AND VENUE OF A TIBETAN SINGER

Serious and thoughtful, the singer Rexi Cairangdan is devoted to recording Tibetan songs for posterity. His home in a rammed earth and timber building across from the Karma Café safeguards Tibetan heritage (such as the old carved windows entrusted to him by families he knows) and offers guests a place of peace. When we visit the singer we are served 'wisdom bread' made in the vast kitchen by a Chinese visitor who assures us the bread's ingredients produce clarity and calm. As we sit in a leafy courtyard enjoying our bread we hear the sound of cymbals and then the pure voice of Rexi Cairangdan singing nostalgically of times in Tibet that are past.

ABOVE:

Old doors and windows were added to the ground floor where traditionally animals are sheltered.

Singer Rexi Cairangdan poses with his antique cymbals.

LEFT:

Tibetan *tigma* cloth is used as a table runner.

A black pottery charcoal burner, made in the nearby village of Nixi, is used to create warmth during cold winter evenings.

OPPOSITE CLOCKWISE:

Typical of houses in Gyalthang, the second storey has a wide wooden balcony facing the courtyard.

A salvaged window frame is used to shelve treasured objects.

A wooden chest used for storing tsampa (ground barley) is converted into a counter and sink.

KUMAON: 360 LETI

The Kumaon region lies in the north Indian hill state of Uttarakhand, a state bordered by Tibet to the north and on the east by Nepal. The traditional houses built in the region's foothills have dry-stack stone walls, mud floors, and *pantangans* (courtyards) of grey stone. A *kholi* (central doorway) is carved with figures of Hindu gods and goddesses and flanked on either side by carved windows. The wood elements are often painted brightly in blue or green, in contrast to the whitewashed, mud-plastered walls. Gently sloping roofs covered with *pataal* (slate) sealed with mud effectively conserve heat in the winter.

Influences on the style of Kumaoni architecture are said to come from Nepal, as once the area was under the Nepalese Gorkha Kingdom. Craftsmen from Gujarat built many of the houses of wealthy landowners, bringing to the region their architectural heritage as well. Local soft timber allowed for the art of woodcarving to become popular.

Set at an altitude of 8,000 feet, 360 Leti is a retreat with a view of the snowy peaks of the Great Himalayan Range. The retreat's four guest pavilions and a main lounge dining area were inspired by local architecture. From here guests walk through oak and rhododendron forests, view a range of stunning mountain peaks and visit the charming Kumaoni villages.

In the Kumaon Valley stone houses have carved and brightly painted timber elements. The guest buildings of 360 Leti reflect local style in proportion and materials. The panelled windows, however, are contemporary and provide splendid Himalayan views.

UTILIZING LOCAL SKILLS AND MATERIALS

CLOCKWISE:

A local mason builds a dry-stack exterior wall with stones from a nearby quarry.

Women porter parts of the timber structure that were made off-site, based on carrying capacity and with respect to the narrow width of mountain trails.

The dining and lounge building serves guests staying in the four cottages. According to the agreement with local people, buildings were kept small so that fields could still be used for farming, and the property would have no concrete construction as it would eventually be returned to them.

The living area of a guest cottage features a fireplace and built-in couch.

RIGHT:

The stone structures of 360 Leti fit into the surrounding landscape and through timber-framed windows offer remarkable views.

360 LETI

The model is practical: local people lease the land for 10 years to the owners of the retreat, who must afterwards return the land. Buildings are to have no concrete construction and be built of minimal size so as to allow continued use of the fields for farming. People who commonly porter materials in the mountains are employed to carry the heavy stones from a quarry 500 metres away. Then the building units are constructed in accordance with the seasonal work calendar. The straight-forward vision of 360 Leti seems unflawed – could it be the new model for sustainable Himalayan resorts?

Indeed the simple complex of buildings (four guest units and a common building for relaxing and dining) fits easily and unobtrusively onto a three-acre, 2,300 metre high ridge. And though a challenge to access (an overnight train from Delhi, more than seven hours by car and an hour's hike along a narrow trail) the resort with its spectacular views is a true destination. The view is unscarred by electric wires. You have the sense of coming upon an archeological site, so embedded are the recent structures in the landscape.

For his client, Shakti Himalaya, Bijoy Jain of Studio Mumbai and his architectural team took several trips to Leti to study vernacular architecture. Built by master masons from the area, indigenous houses measure 3 x 5 metres and have thick stone walls. Interior walls are insulated with a layer of mud, lime, and dung plaster. The buildings are elevated 1.5 metres above the ground, allowing space for animals underneath and also a convenient means to warm the buildings from below.

The local masons were consulted on the final design of five separate guest structures and they built the foundations and the dry stacked stone walls. Studio Mumbai's own team of carpenters camped out at the site and during a period of three months incorporated the timber frames, glass, and roof structure. These elements had been designed and built earlier with the foreknowledge that porters would need to carry them along the narrow walking track that leads to the ridge.

When finished, recycled stone floors were laid and timber was oiled. The resulting rooms have simple wood and stone furnishings softened by natural-coloured textiles. Much of the seating is built-in. A table nearby the fireplace is a simple slab of stone, while a wooden couch is set into a glass-panelled wall. As the walls of glass allow magnificent views of the mountains beyond, the guest feels little barrier to the landscape. The buildings nestle into the ground as if to say, let us not interrupt: observe the mountains, find the trails, and learn the stars at night.

Part 5
Style in the
Kathmandu
Valley

It is hard to imagine that Kathmandu Valley was not reachable by a motor road before 1956 – and until then cars were lifted by more than sixty porters up an old trading route from India. Today it is well known that the streets of Kathmandu are choked with traffic, its holy river (the Bagmati) severely polluted, and its water and electricity are scarce. Yet the creative life of the city has never diminished and Kathmandu pulses with colour and music like never before. Within the city are families who have nurtured artistic skills for hundreds of years: hence many Newar traditions of pottery, brassware, gold and silver, painting, brick masonry, wood and stone carving, still thrive. At the same time there are new developments in conceptual art, music, film, and theatre. In the field of design, Nepal's crafts traditions are also taking new forms through the exchange of ideas between Nepalese designers and artisans as well as a number of foreign designers who have travelled to or resided in Nepal.

In the first chapter, 'Designers meet Artisans', we look at different crafts produced by Nepalese, Tibetan, and Western designers in Nepal, as well as the unique homes created by a number of these designers. The chapter 'After the Ranas' examines how neo-classical Kathmandu Valley architecture is now adapted for life in the 21st century. 'Living in Bhaktapur' provides a glimpse into the lifestyles of two long-term foreign residents, an architect and a musician, whose homes and gardens manifest their passion for traditional Himalayan art and design. The final chapter, 'Living in Patan' shows how the traditional city of Patan preserves its tremendous artistic heritage. Blending old and new, local and imported aesthetics, the styles that are presented in these pages perpetuate the unique identity of the Kathmandu Valley.

At Pipalbot, a contemporary lifestyle store in Kathmandu, giant balls of yarn and a loom complement a display of contemporary rugs that interpret paintings by Bangkok-based artist Peter Delahaye.

DESIGNERS MEET ARTISANS

Many of the private homes created in the Kathmandu Valley draw upon traditional styles and craftsmanship, creating artful sanctuaries within the mayhem of city life. Diverse spiritual beliefs and practices are reflected in a variety of home altars. Some homes are like small museums of Asian art and objects collected with care over time. They may also serve as studios where artists, designers, writers, and musicians are inspired to create anew.

In small workshops on back streets and alleys, traditional artisans and contemporary designers meet and create together. The results of their synergy can be enjoyed in retail spaces such as Pipalbot, described in the following pages.

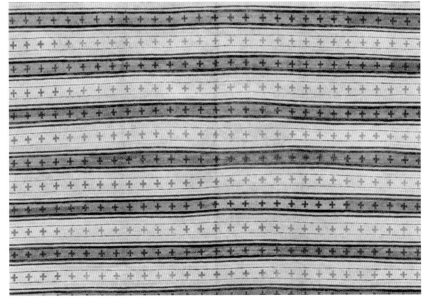

LEFT FROM TOP:

In a kaleidoscopic composition representing flashing jewels, Pasang Tsering juxtaposes the different stripe combinations of apron cloth woven in Lhasa, Nyalam, Dhingri, Lhatse, and Mount Kailash.

Detail of a carpet by Stephanie Odegard entitled *Yunglock Thickma*. The carpet is inspired by Tibetan wool cloth that is stamped with a cross motif.

Warm orange colours contrast shades of indigo blue in a carpet by Odegard entitled *Pangden Sherab*. The design of the carpet is derived from the traditional Tibetan striped apron called pangden.

OPPOSITE:

In the home of a Kathmandu couple who design carpets and cashmere shawls, an old Tibetan saddle sits beside a carpet hand-woven with silk and wild nettle. Its design was inspired by a traditional Tibetan saddle carpet. Cashmere shawls are hung on a ladder that leans against the wall.

PIPALBOT

The name 'Pipalbot' translates as 'Pipul tree' (the sacred tree under which Buddha attained enlightenment) and also connotes a gathering place for Kathmandu people. Pipalbot is a venue designed by Diki Ongmo and Tim Linkins, who honed their unique aesthetic in Tibet Sydney, a contemporary lifestyle store in Australia. Pipalbot brings Diki's Tibetan background and design skills together with Tim's knowledge of cutting-edge architecture, art, and photography. As they had hoped, they have succeeded in bringing to Kathmandu 'a breath of fresh air'. Here, Nepal's ancient craft traditions are energized with contemporary design in a space that has been renovated with great care and originality.

A source of inspiration for their project was the work of Alvar Aalto, the Finnish architect who designed furniture and objects. The couple was also taken by the inventive transformation of old buildings by Italian architect Carlo Scarpa. Tim, a professional architecture photographer, wondered, "The design ideas collected from Australia and Europe – how would they translate in Nepal?"

Pipalbot is housed in Babar Mahal Revisited, a complex of shops and restaurants designed in a classic Rana-era style. With consultation between Tim, the Sydney-based architect Timothy Hill, and New York-based designer Shane Powers, the area Pipalbot occupies was transformed to improve light and acoustics and to create the openness Tim and Diki required to achieve their vision. Skylights allowed light in from above, while new floors were created with white cement whose patina suggests a much older surface. A timber wall was added to the thin cement walls, increasing their depth, providing hanging space and absorbing echoes. The resulting deep window wells resemble windows of more ancient buildings and scoop in the exterior light. Tim notes how the small change of wrapping a timber screen around the interior space suggests 'solidity, groundedness, a sense of being here forever' just as one experiences in a Tibetan monastery.

The exterior façade of Babar Mahal Revisited, the Rana-style shopping complex that houses Pipalbot.

From the traditional exterior you enter through a door frame (painted in the bright hue of orange tikka powder) to a world that Tim likens to an engaging landscape. This is not just a store displaying commercial merchandise. You can sit on the couch and drink tea, or at the long tiled dining table to enjoy unique fusion meals and meet people who have emerged from the city's different points and social circles. All of Pipalbot evolves from one clear vision of a space that both invites and gives. The healthy, artfully presented food is at one with the tasteful cashmere clothing, the cheerful carpets Diki has designed, and the original metalwork by Götz Hagmüller and Wendy Marston. Together, the combination of elements creates an impression of cheerful elegance. But there is more: at night Pipalbot is a venue for films, a teaching by a well-known Rinpoche, or a meditation class. On a full-moon night, guests may be found listening to Indian classical music, comfortably seated on old Tibetan carpets.

At first Tim and Diki chose favourite traditional craftspeople to exhibit their wares, but now craftspeople come to them. At Pipalbot they gain new ideas, coming out of their traditional 'craft zone'. Heera Didi is one craftswoman who made traditional cane products and now is filling customer orders for new airy bulb-shaped hanging lamps.

Tim describes their space as a sanctuary where you can leave the traffic, enjoy a cup of tea, and find pleasure in seeing the latest crafts delivered by local craftspeople. Perhaps, too, you make a new friend at the long table (over a bowl of corn soup with chive oil, or a dish of chrysanthemum sushi). A view through the window to the trees reminds you that nature is nearby. The cup for tea was hand-made in nearby Thimi, the tray in Bhaktapur. The green tea is organic. Everything in Pipalbot connects: past and present, city and nature, far and near.

OPPOSITE CLOCKWISE:

Bright threads used in Buddhist temple hangings are used in the store's display.

Floor cushions made from hand-knotted silk carpets are stacked behind a luminous back-painted glass table. Chairs are made of dyed and woven papyrus.

A carpet designed by Diki Ongmo was inspired by pompoms used for yarn samples and a famous painting by Damien Hirst.

At the communal table, monks from the monastery of Chökyi Nyima Rinpoche recite prayers for removing obstacles at Pipalbot.

ABOVE:

Carpets of Diki Ongmo's design are made in Nepal. The carpet in the centre has a classic Tibetan peony motif given a contemporary edge. The relief effect is made by playing with pile height. A split bamboo lamp designed by Pipalbot and produced by Heera Didi hangs in the foreground.

The mosaic tiles on the communal dining table create a reflective surface increasing light at the end of the room. Brassware is produced in Patan and turned wooden bowls are from Bhutan. In remodelling the room, the Rana-style arched upper windows, which had been covered over, were reinstated.

Award-winning light decorations by Dutch designer Tord Boontje hang with a locally-made lampshade of bamboo. A wooden statue from Nepal sits amongst carpets of Islamic inspiration and a traditional Tibetan dragon carpet. In a neutral space, Pipalbot mixes disparate things to show how they work together.

Ceramics designed by Shane Powers and produced by Thimi Ceramics line the shelves of an open kitchen that also becomes a display space. Brass lamps are by Götz Hagmüller.

An antique Tibetan saddle blanket with peony motifs in shades of indigo blue lies on a wicker lounge chair made in Nepal.

THIMI CERAMICS

The historic Kathmandu Valley town of Thimi is the home of about 10,000 potters, all members of the Newar potter caste 'Prajapati'. In the early 1980s, many of the potter families participated in a development project headed by American ceramics expert James Danisch that taught many of them to glaze pottery for the first time. Shanta and Laxmi Kumar Prajapati have led a workshop named 'Thimi Ceramics' to become the first producers of stoneware in Nepal. The brothers worked in close cooperation with American potter Ani Kasten, who assisted development of a new range of glazes using local materials, and designed a line of pottery that is now exported around the world. 'Remnants' is the word Ani uses to describe some of the gentle, timeless forms in her own work. While very contemporary, the shapes made in Thimi also look so natural that they might have already existed for many years.

ANI KASTEN

The potters I worked with in Thimi had mostly been making ceramics since a very young age (often 6, 7 or 8 years old was when people had begun to work with clay, helping their parents in the workshop). This meant that the men I was working with who were in their 20s and 30s were already masters of their craft. The precision and skill was incredible for me to see. But I could also see that their future in Nepal was uncertain unless there could be greater appreciation for pottery and the status of potters (who are low caste) was raised. It was my vision to bring my aesthetic sensibility in relation to ceramics as an incredible art form with unlimited possibility, and meet it with the high level of skill present in Thimi, in hopes of elevating the level of the ceramic product they were able to produce.

I wanted to help them to innovate but at the same time keep grounded to the tradition of simple, utilitarian pottery that has always been produced in Thimi. This was an idea that informed my designs as I began to create table settings for them to make. My training with British potter Rupert Spira was extremely valuable to me, as he taught me to pare down my forms. His own ceramics were completely minimal, and he didn't tolerate anything in the work that was inessential. This was a perfect aesthetic philosophy to bring to my colleagues in Thimi because their traditional pottery was similarly unadorned, and based only on utility. My job in working with the Thimi potters was to reveal how great beauty could reside in such simplicity of design. We had to hone the skill and design and make form and beauty as much a focus as utility.

Bowls in earth hues are designed by Ani Kasten and produced in Thimi where Ani helped to spur the development of stoneware.

SHANE POWERS

Similar to the West's increasingly powerful 'farm to table' idea, our idea for Pipalbot was that it would be 'artisan to shop'. All of the products sold at Pipalbot are made within a 30-mile radius of the city. Every day of my two months' stay was filled with visits to the artisans, slowly getting to know them and the materials they work with. I was inspired by the materials they considered 'poor', that which they see as just plain and everyday, and often I was drawn to the honest and straightforward materials they pushed to the back of their workshops. Such was the case with the ceramic studio we visited in Thimi, near the ancient city of Bhaktapur. Outside of the studio I spotted rows and rows of tiles made of a light earthy pink clay glazed with traditional Nepali motifs. I became obsessed with the colour of the clay usually used for products where the clay is hidden, and immediately saw the shapes of the ceramics I wanted to produce: soft and round like the human body but structured and iconic like temples from antiquity or the distant future. A light terracotta-coloured tea set is composed of nine pieces unglazed on the outside, but finished with a glossy, opaque white glaze on the inside. The contrast of the dry porous exterior and the glazed interior is both sensual to the sight and touch. Drinking from the cups you smell the faintest hint of clay. It chips beautifully and darkens with use.

The kind of opportunity I had in Thimi, and the opportunity I had with artisans making a set of brass cutlery, are only the tip of the iceberg in a place where artisans are still making things every day by hand, often right in the back of the shops on the streets. Ideas emerge uncontrollably when people still share a passion for working with their hands. Food, craft, and cultural traditions keep these skills vibrant.

Tea cups with elemental forms are designed by Shane Powers and made in Thimi by traditional potters.

COUNTRY FIBERS FOR URBAN LIVING

Throughout the hills and valleys of the Himalayan region people are adept at using local fibers to weave baskets and mats for every day use. Shyam Badan Shrestha formed Weave Fiber Nepal to extend the possibilities of traditional fiber weaving and employ rural people. With its mud-coloured walls, her store in Kathmandu evokes a village house in Nepal where people gather to weave thatch, mats, and baskets. Woven into elemental forms with rice husk, papyrus and a range of other indigenous fibers, Shyam's products now bring the soft beauty of the countryside into contemporary homes throughout Kathmandu.

FROM TOPI TO TABLES: DHAKA WEAVES

A popular cloth of Nepal's middle hills is called 'Dhaka'. The colourful cotton cloth utilizing a complex tapestry weave is used for men's caps (*topi*), women's side-closing blouses and for blankets to swaddle babies. Today a group of weavers, led by Rita Thapa and her daughter Prativa, have brought Dhaka cloth to new heights through their company, Dhaka Weaves. The vibrant colours and patterns of Prativa's designs are used in a range of items for home décor, as seen in these photos of Dhaka cloth runners on Kathmandu tables.

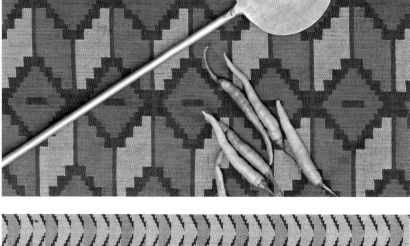

OPPOSITE PAGE:

Rice husk, papyrus and other natural fibers are used to weave the contemporary products by Weave Fiber Nepal.

THIS PAGE:

The patterns in textiles produced by Dhaka Weaves are derived from the traditional patterns of the topi, a cap popularly worn by men in Nepal.

LIGHTING THE CLOUDS

In Babar Mahal Revisited, light emanates from clouds and lotuses that float on the wall in a little store called Paper Moon. These and other paper lampshades are inspired by the motifs and patterns in the Himalayan cultures that Marina Shrestha has absorbed over many years. Settled in Nepal since 1980, Marina has created a dynamic company called Marina Paper that builds on Nepal's native papermaking tradition. Nepal is known for its unique paper that uses the renewable daphne plant, as well as its growing industry making recycled papers. Marina has drawn on her training in France as an architect to produce expertly designed paper products that include window shades, photo frames, and small shrines that are found in homes throughout Kathmandu.

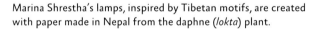

Marina Shrestha's lamps, inspired by Tibetan motifs, are created with paper made in Nepal from the daphne (*lokta*) plant.

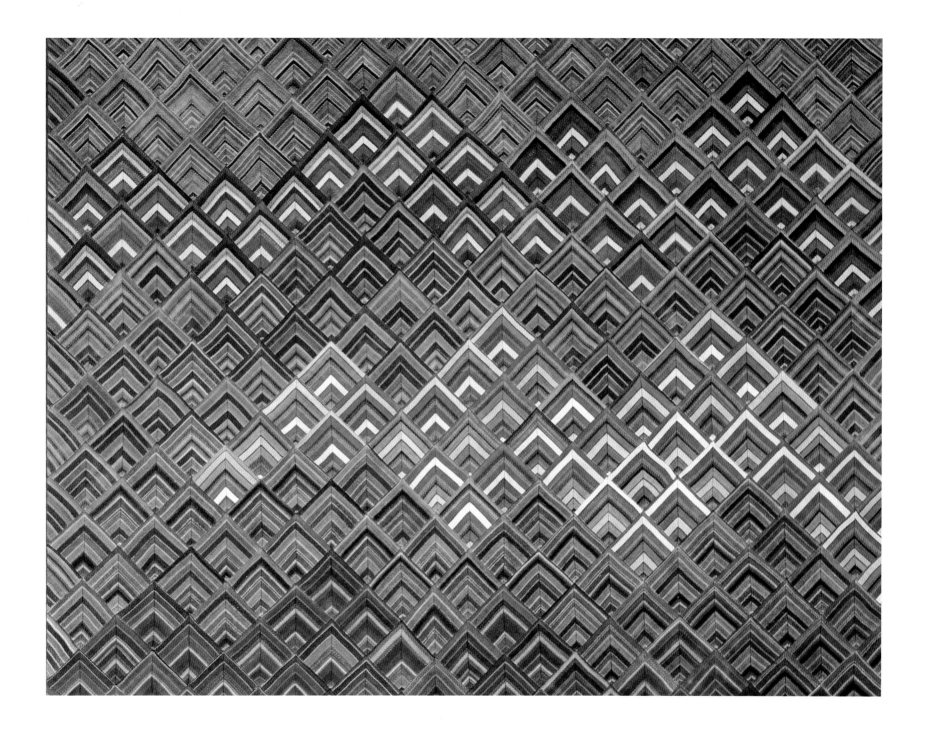

THE PANGDEN:
A VIBRANT TEXTILE REBORN

Pangden are the aprons worn by women of Tibetan heritage over their long dresses or *chuba*. As the most important decorative element of a woman's clothing, the pangden serves to identify her community or region and to indicate her marital status.

The colours of sheep wool yarn used in the weft are created by natural and chemical dyes. Madder (for red), rhubarb root (for orange and yellow), and indigo are common natural dye materials, while a popular hot pink is made with chemical powder. On a simple 1-2 shaft hand-made wooden loom, the dyed yarn is woven in numerous stripe combinations that are usually memorized. Once taken off the loom, the cloth is held to a flame, section by section, to burn off the excess fuzz and thereby create a smooth finish. Three lengths of cloth are hand-stitched together to make an apron. Colours are bold and stripes are not matched at the seams. Today the vibrant pangden has a modern look and has become an inspiration for new exciting textiles and carpets.

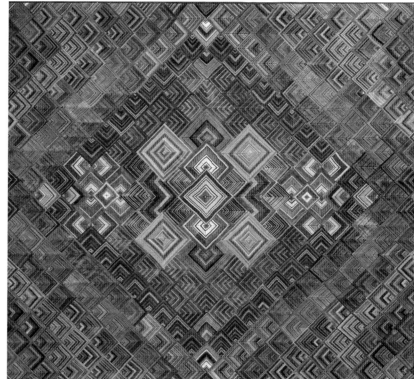

REINVENTING A TIBETAN TRADITION

When he was born in Lhasa in 1959, Pasang Tsering's parents, who were professional dyers, swaddled him in tie-dyed cloth. Just after the Cultural Revolution, his family came to live in Bouddhanath, a Tibetan settlement in Kathmandu. Pasang describes Bouddha as "a distributer of an engine – you encountered everyone from traditional people to Westerners – it was a big university." It was here that he discovered and developed a new Tibetan art form.

Pasang is passionate as he talks about the Tibet of his childhood and the near impossibility today of preserving a traditional way of life. At first he worked only restoring old textiles. Then after some years he felt he should make things from the old and often irreparable materials. He loved how each colour scheme and stripe pattern had its own identity – it was easy to know if a textile came from Tingri or Shigatse in Tibet, or Dolpo in Nepal. Even nomads as far as Ladakh began to bring him textiles, never imagining how the textiles would be transformed.

Having excelled at painting in his youth, and with a strong inherited sense of colour, he began to play with ways to cut aprons to make a square cover for a cushion. Gradually his designs with apron cloth grew more complex, contrasting the patterns of cloth woven in different Tibetan regions and hence capturing the energy from many different weavers.

"Traditional textile is imbued with its own life that pulls you back into time and slows you down. A textile retains its history, colour, and the whole reason it was made," explains Pasang, and points to his shirt. "Its texture has a life and richness and it speaks to us differently than an Adidas T-shirt."

Pasang conceives the design and four other employees sew. The designs include a universal mandala, where the indigo background (reused cloth from a Tibetan *chuba*) becomes the space of the universe. In his version of an endless knot, a central mandala is framed by four lotus petal corners in perfect kaleidoscopic symmetry. For a magnificent landscape piece entitled *The Mountain and Sun*, carefully selected stripes create the effect of light moving across several mountain ranges.

He describes his work as "genuine Tibetan art given a new shape to sustain it into the 21st century." Yet with both acceptance and regret, he adds, "What I am doing can't go on for very long." The tradition of weaving aprons may not last another generation.

"Like a rainbow, my work is now and will be gone."

LEFT:

In *Simple Mandala in the Shadow of Samsara,* the universal mandala floats on a field of indigo-dyed wool cloth.

ABOVE:

Pangden from six Tibetan regions are used to depict the gems of a *ga'u*, a Tibetan amulet necklace.

ABOVE RIGHT:

A composition representing Tantric ritual objects including a dorje and cymbals.

PANGDEN AMA AND PANGDEN PLATEAU

Inspired by old Tibetan carpets and textiles of many styles, Stephanie Odegard began designing modern Tibetan carpets in 1986 and soon gained international recognition for her superbly designed and woven carpets from Nepal. Her company Odegard Inc. produces carpets that incorporate many of the world's great motifs and patterns. Some of her most striking and best-selling carpets continue to be based on traditional Tibetan pangden. She has also developed unique rugs derived from the Tibetan *methok* (flower), *shomik* (square) and *belak* (frog's feet) patterns, but the pangden, which she describes as 'timeless', remains a signature Odegard pattern.

Odegard enjoys the energy produced by unmatched stripes and believes that some of the weavers have 'a taste and sensitivity to colour' that is very similar to her own. She produced her first pangden carpet in 1989, which was designed by Barbara Silverstein and named *Pangden Ama*

(*ama* means 'mother'). The success of *Pangden Ama* generated another 15 different pangden carpets. "I started to identify pangden that I liked on Tibetan women in New York City, Kathmandu, and Lhasa, and I would ask each woman if I could photograph her and borrow her pangden to copy for putting into carpet designs," Odegard explains. "I always named each pangden after the owner of the original pangden."

Like traditional pangden, the carpets employ a mix of rich colours in stripes of varied widths. The carpets pretend to be formed by three panels stitched together, just like traditional aprons, but in some pieces, such as the carpets named *Pangden Plateau* and *Tiers shown in Cerulean*, the stripes have become blocks and have shifted sideways out of their standard three columns. The composition is reminiscent of the shapes made by the small fields that are farmed individually in Himalayan valleys.

RIGHT:

Typically, a pangden contrasts
warm and cool colours. Odegard's
first pangden carpet, named
Pangden Ama, has three columns of
contrasting stripes in deep hues.

OPPOSITE LEFT:

The columns of stripes in *Pangden
Multi II* are bright and bold.

OPPOSITE RIGHT:

In a carpet named *Tiers shown in
Cerulean* muted blocks of colour
have shifted out of the regular
columns of earlier pangden carpets.

CASHMERE PERFECTION: A SMALL WEAVING WORKSHOP AIMS HIGH

With each of his endeavours, Christopher Giercke has used his tremendous creative energy to achieve a standard of excellence. He has been a child film star in East Germany and a producer of important films on Himalayan Buddhism. Now he divides his time between his horse polo camp in Mongolia (the native home of his wife Enkhe), Europe, and Nepal. He has also been able to produce some of the Himalayas' finest quality cashmere shawls, blankets, and felt carpets (Hermes being but one of his prestigious clients).

Christopher explains that he has always been involved in 'crafting', whether the medium was film or yarn. "You need time, you need to do what you feel is right. In Mongolia I had the quality raw material, and in Nepal there was the crafting heritage – the Newars can do anything." His airy, light-filled weaving workshop in Nepal is in itself a work of art, with its steel frame structure painted azure blue and white ceiling curtains. Here one finds a master warper winding cashmere yarn on an immense blue warping drum, a group of expert tailors blanket-stitching the edges of a natural coloured cashmere blanket, a master dyer hanging to dry 200 finely-woven shawls dyed ruby red, and two Mongolian experts carding by hand Mongolian wool to make a magnificently soft felt carpet.

He and Enkhe use their woven products in their tasteful, minimally decorated home. White felt sitting rugs surround a low table in the bedroom and the bed is covered with white cashmere. The staircase has a runner with naturally dyed wool. The house, like their products, reflects an appreciation for materials that are authentic and natural.

LEFT:

Naturally dyed skeins of sheep wool.

Tibetan wooden bowls turned upside-down to show their silver decoration, and a photograph of Christopher Giercke.

Warp ends on a workshop loom.

OPPOSITE:

A stairway runner combines several panels of hand-woven naturally coloured sheep wool cloth.

Simple rectangles of white cashmere felt create seating around a low table.

Dark wooden objects and furnishings contrast the white cotton, wool, and cashmere used throughout the home.

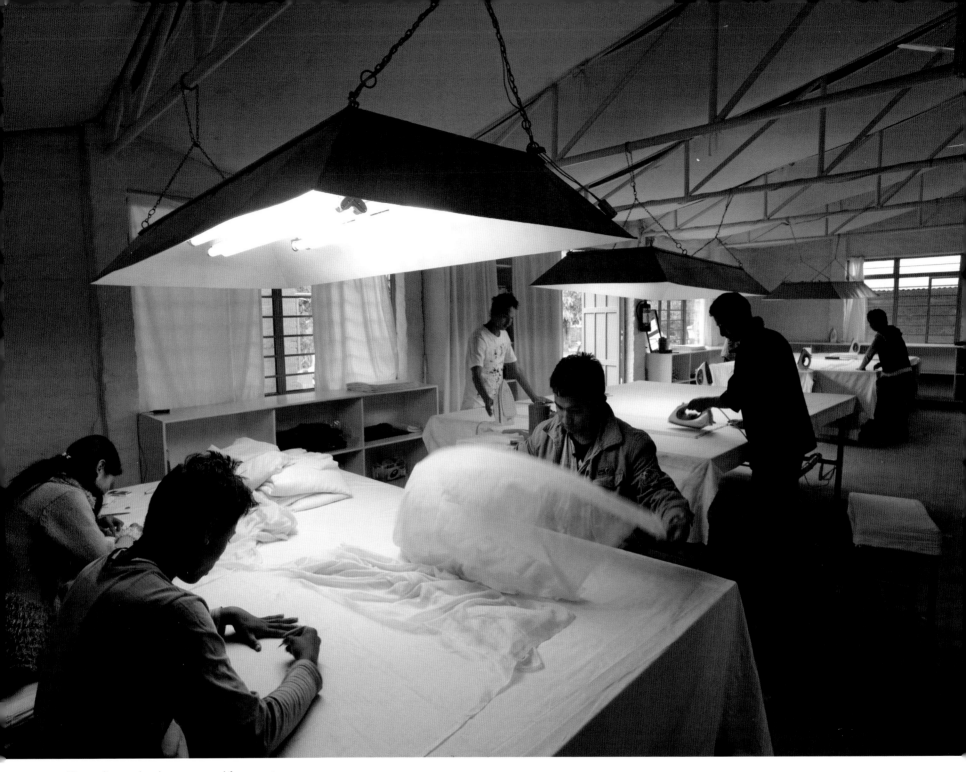

Fine cashmere shawls are prepared for export
in a clean and airy finishing room.

OPPOSITE:

The weaving workshop with painted blue equipment and roof
structure. White cotton curtains under the corrugated metal
roof lighten the room.

Mongolian cashmere being prepared for felting.

The Master Weaver on his giant loom.

The ringed toes of a weaver's feet on her loom's blue treadles.

Dyed cashmere shawls dry on a line.

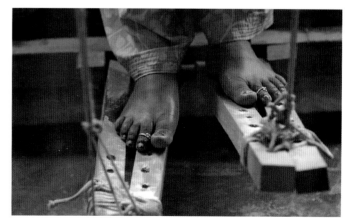

MUSKHANE: A FELT STORY

Felt has long been made and used traditionally in the Himalayas for items such as hats, jackets, mattresses, saddle blankets, and tents. Production of felt by commercial artisans in Nepal grew in the 1990s. In 2002 a French couple, Thierry and Valerie Billot, decided to create an ethical business to support Nepali artisans – particularly producers of felt – and to connect them to the rest of the world. Passionate about living and travelling in Nepal, each of their collections for their company, Muskhane, absorbs the experiences from their latest family sojourn. Valerie finds sources of inspiration all around: "Mineral colours from lower Mustang, bright colours from tikka powder or from saris... it depends on my mood, and the places I have just visited." Mustang is clearly the influence in one series of carpets with bold earth colours, which may be hung on the wall like abstract paintings. The colours of rugs and cushions suggest the earth colours of house walls, the pastels created by lime wash, or the deep yellows and reds of monks' robes.

Rugs and cushions that make for comfortable floor seating are a feature of Valerie and Thierry's Kathmandu house. *Muskhane* means 'smile' in Nepali, and many of Muskhane's felt products are notably playful and upbeat. A lighthearted combination of ochre and deep pink is predominant throughout their open ground-floor space, which includes a living room separated from the dining area by a wide arch reminiscent of a moon gate. Numerous round felt carpets add both warmth and fun to the cool stone paving. Simple lampshades made of sheets of white or yellow handmade paper are also products of Muskhane. The living room evokes the colourful atmosphere of a Kathmandu market: colours reflect turmeric, chili, tikka powder, incense, garlands of marigolds, and other bright hues of flower petals collected for offerings.

The Billot's living room is decorated with Muskhane's felt cushions and carpets as well as sitting cushions made of Tibetan *nambu* cloth. The colours of turmeric and Tibetan monks' robes provided Valerie with design inspiration.

CLOCKWISE:

Felt carpets are inspired by the earth colours used on the walls of houses and temples in Mustang, Nepal.

Cushions and throws made of Tibetan wool nambu cloth are embellished with pompoms. Flowers float in a traditional brass vessel made in Nepal. Shiva and Parvati, framed in hand-made paper, look on from the wall.

Coloured cushions brighten up an outdoor bench.

CLOCKWISE:

Rugs and cushions, turmeric yellow and deep red, create a cheerful ambience in the Billot's open living and dining space. Simple Nepali paper lampshades are also produced by Muskhane. The striking wall hanging is designed by Pasang Tsering using Tibetan apron cloth.

Muskhane's felt cushions, with colours inspired by Nepal's tikka powders, spices, and flower offerings, offer comfortable seating on a wooden bench.

A MOVEABLE HOUSE

In the booming cityscape of Kathmandu, people are searching for quiet living spaces. When Leslie Shackleford, artist and designer of jewellery and carpets, learned she had to move again, she decided she should build a moveable house that she could take with her, whether she lived in Patan, Kathmandu or out in the countryside. She came up with a solution that was quick and inexpensive: she would partition a big residential compound she had under lease, rent out the large family house and build a temporary dwelling where there was a pond and Newar-style resthouse (*pati*) for entertaining guests. She contacted Suresh Shrestha who is known for his work on the Patan Museum and for designing and building small family homes in the Kathmandu Valley. Suresh built the house with steel, glass, clapboard, and corrugated steel for the roof. Sheltered by trees, the house sits on steel legs with its French doors opening out over the pond toward the pati. Furnishings are simple and include Leslie's favourite pieces of Tibetan furniture, rugs she has designed based on traditional Tibetan carpets, and storage units for her artwork. Her four dogs rescued from Kathmandu streets amble in and out. Light pours through the branches of trees, dappling everything. Within the walls of her glass house she has found peace and calm and plenty of privacy.

Glass doors of the bedroom and living room open out to a fish pond and a secluded garden.

CLOCKWISE:

A view from the bedroom to the kitchen. The white clapboard wall has small shutters below the roof, allowing cross-ventilation.

A pangden produced in Tibet adds a dash of bold colour.

The pati, built in traditional Newar style, offers a pleasant alternative space for reading or entertaining.

OPPOSITE CLOCKWISE:

A comfortable seating area combines cotton and silk cushions, a low Tibetan table and a rug produced by Leslie that follows a traditional Tibetan pattern.

Doors of the bedroom and living room open to a stone patio and fish pond.

A glass-covered table displays artifacts, photos, sketches, and paint brushes.

ROOM WITH A VIEW:
A COUPLE DESIGNS FROM THEIR
MOUNTAINSIDE HOME

As if up to a Tibetan temple you climb to a house that is sheltered amongst trees and feels far from the sprawling city in the Kathmandu Valley below. Entering the main rear door, you have an instant view through the house and out again through glass doors that face onto the entire Valley.

The owners of this house, a Tibetan carpet producer and his wife, a Scandinavian designer, have mastered the art of living minimally. A huge open living room is demarcated invisibly into neat spaces for the dining table, desk, sofa, and master bed. The whites and off-whites that predominate in this light-filled room are punctuated with a vase of red orchids, a turquoise-coloured Eames chair, and numerous cashmere shawls, including one that is the beautiful green-blue colour of a clear Tibetan lake. The hand-loomed shawls and the subtle carpets are produced in their workshop nearby. Some of the carpets are made with *allo* (wild nettle) and silk. The Himalayan giant nettle grows at 1200-3000 metres throughout Nepal and is traditionally harvested and processed by hand. Carpets made with allo wear well and fade attractively with time. Most recently the couple have used nettle and silk in the reinvention of saddle carpets with traditional patterns.

Their design collaboration began in the early years of their marriage, after realizing they could put to use their knowledge of and interest in indigenous Himalayan crafts. His Tibetan family provided support and inspiration with their hands-on knowledge of weaving techniques, sourcing of wool and experience in making a range of traditional textiles. Meanwhile, their house was built with the shared desire of an open and tranquil space that was harmonious with the surrounding natural beauty. This vision was sketched in late nights at their drawing table, while in the building stage, adjustments were made that matched the practical experience of local brick layers and carpenters. The blending of sophisticated design with time-tried techniques and materials has resulted in a graceful yet solid structure that is both home and workplace.

The open living and work space, with glass doors to a wide balcony, is heated by a wood-burning stove. The couple's throws, shawls, and soft carpets (hand-woven with cashmere, silk and wild nettle) create warmth in the home as well.

CLOCKWISE:

Cashmere shawls are draped over chairs ready for use during cool evenings.

The surrounding forested hills are seen through a picture window. The bed, topped with furs and throws, rests on a base of old carved beams.

Locally made wicker chairs mix with Eames chairs at the simple dining table. Glass doors open to a wide terrace.

OPPOSITE:

A new silk and allo version of a traditional Tibetan saddle carpet lies at the entry to the kitchen.

Silk kata are tied to a pillar to bless the house.

Exterior walls are brick-coloured cement. This shawl with earth-tone stripes is woven with silk and Tibetan cashmere.

In the daytime, the couple uses the open space to present their textiles to clients or even to sketch new designs directly on the concrete floor with chalk. Cashmere and wool samples are spread over the furniture and the two dogs, a Tibetan Mastiff and a Lhasa Apso, help to test the durability of the weaves. In the evening, the space becomes private again, with time to contemplate on the terrace at sunset or in front of the wood stove. It is in the pragmatic use of space that the owners see their house as truly Himalayan: it is not meant to be an after-office place for leisure, but rather a space of purposeful activity that accommodates many different kinds of people throughout the day, like, the owners say, 'a farmer's house'.

Views of the solid brick library building from east and west. The architect incorporated both flat and barrel vaulted roof shapes, an idea that was novel at the time. This building used to contain three guest apartments that were recently combined to house the research centre with a library.

OPPOSITE:

The large northern-facing round window provides subtle light for the reading room. After forty years the doors and windows were replaced with simple welded steel frames.

TARAGAON: REVIVING THE VALLEY'S MODERN ARCHITECTURE

The Taragaon Hotel, designed by Austrian architect Carl Pruscha in 1972, exemplifies some of the most distinctive modern architecture in the Kathmandu Valley. While most restoration projects in the Valley focus on architecture hundreds of years old, the Taragaon, after years of disuse, has been converted into spaces for art exhibitions, a café, and specialty shops. A permanent exhibit highlights contributions of international Kathmandu residents and includes works by a number of noted photographers and architects.

Pruscha's design had been inspired by early Buddhist architecture. When entering the complex of buildings made with local brick one has the sense of coming upon an excavation of a lost historical site, so elemental are the forms. In the restoration effort, architects Niels Gutschow and Thomas Schrom retained the original exteriors, while making necessary changes to the interiors, such as the removal of walls that used to separate guest apartments. The new Taragaon highlights the importance of both preserving and creating attractive modern architecture in the Kathmandu Valley.

AFTER THE RANAS

During the Rana dynasty (1846–1951) Nepal was ruled by members of the extended Rana family who made the position of prime minister hereditary. The Ranas are remembered with mixed admiration for their love of European art and culture and for a new form of architecture that took root in the Kathmandu Valley under their rule. Borrowing neo-classical European style, the Ranas built themselves grand white stucco palaces and imported crystal chandeliers, marble tables, and other sumptuous furnishings. Local people imitated the architectural style in urban and village houses of smaller proportions, using local exposed brick with red mortar pointing, painting window frames white, and adorning walls with charming plaster ornamentation.

Rana style has been recreated in Babar Mahal Revisited, a complex of shops and restaurants that transforms and extends the carriage house and cowsheds that belonged to a Rana palace. The style has also been revived and reinterpreted in the Garden of Dreams, a garden originally conceived by Kaiser Shumsher Rana on the grounds of his palace, Keshar Mahal. Today, traditional Rana homes are being pulled down to make way for modern apartment buildings: here we record for posterity the home of Barbara Adams that she lovingly struggles to preserve. And in a positive development, a Rana building was recently preserved and renovated by Pipalbot's Tim Linkins to make a clean, smart new space for a trekking office.

The Keshar Mahal Palace was built by Bir Shumsher in 1885 and was the residence until 1964 of Kaiser Shumsher Rana who created an extensive library as well as a renowned garden. The opulent neo-classical interiors are decorated with plaster friezes and massive portraits of the Rana rulers. Ceilings are painted pressed tin and floors are marble tile. Trophies from hunting expeditions in Nepal combine with furniture and chandeliers imported from Europe.

CONVERSION OF A RANA PALACE

When the owner of an old Rana building wanted to convert it into the offices of a trekking company, he consulted Tim Linkins, creator of the lifestyle store, Pipalbot. The building had the attractive feature that its walls were two and a half feet wide and of huge scale, but it needed opening up to bring in light and to connect separate spaces.

"Before renovating," Linkins recounts, "the building was dark and workers even felt it was haunted. People would get lost within the vast building, the top floor being so dark one needed a torch. So it was necessary to gut it."

The false ceiling was pulled out and a steel truss created to support the roof. The new lighter top-floor meeting room, divided by a blade wall, became the brightest space in the building. In other parts of the building, with more light added, interior details could be better appreciated. Wooden doors were kept simple, and the interiors were painted white. Old French doors were retained and repainted without their typical black or green trim.

CLOCKWISE:

The *gupt baithak* (secret sitting room) in Jeevan SJB Rana's house. The interior is still preserved today.

The façade of the Rana building housing the trekking office.

Lighter stairways allowed for a greater vista and for spaces to connect in a more generous way.

OPPOSITE:

The Rana-era entranceway had been taken up with a heavy wooden stair, blocking easy circulation in the building. Removing the stair allowed for the light well that illuminates the new reception desk.

In the ballroom, Barbara sits below a silk brocade textile coming from Tibet. Carpets are Chinese and the oil lamps Nepalese.

A view to Barbara's work room with Tibetan carpets and Newar brass pots.

OPPOSITE:

Barbara's home displays her unique collection of arts and crafts from around Asia.

A RANA HOME, BELOVED

Barbara Adams' history in Kathmandu spans fifty years, beginning when she was a young and daring blond-haired journalist and consort to a Nepalese royal prince. Now she is one of the wise elders of Kathmandu, with flowing long white hair and her white Sunbeam Alpine convertible parked beside the entrance of her rambling Rana-era house. Today she laughs that she has now been a resident of Nepal "longer than three-quarters of the Nepali population".

Barbara came to Nepal in 1961 to write an article about Queen Elizabeth's visit to Nepal, fell in love with the country and a prince, and stayed. Her house reflects a life richly lived: photos on her wall range from those of Barbara with Jimmy Carter to Barbara with many of Nepal's prominent politicians. Also seen in her home are clay images of King Birendra and Queen Aishwarya, victims of the royal massacre in 2001 and both portrayed in clay by local potters. She recalls, "In 1988 the Queen had me put under house arrest and then thrown out of Nepal. Ten years later, when the democratically elected Prime Minister also had me thrown out, the King graciously brought me back in. Therefore both the King and Queen are part of my history."

The house displays an eclectic mix of village crafts (such as the rough-hewn wooden bowls and striped textiles of Nepal's mountainous regions), Newar brassware, and European-inspired luxury items of the Rana era. "I always loved beautiful things – I could either afford to travel or to collect," Barbara explains. As her collections grew, so they filled her house. Most of Barbara's collection of Bhutanese textiles, found in the seventies while prowling Kathmandu's bazaars, now resides in the Textile Museum of Bhutan.

Her profound experience in Asia is perhaps best reflected in a chandeliered chamber with marble floors originally used as a ballroom. In Barbara's time it would hold Russian gypsy dance parties, holiday celebrations with Christmas trees reaching to the pressed tin ceiling, and student groups who came to hear her lecture about life in Nepal fifty years ago. The room features two pianos that came to her from two well-known foreign denizens of Kathmandu, defying a friend's admonishment that 'less is more'. One piano top is covered by an antique Kashmir shawl and displays a rustic basket from Nepal's southern Tharu peoples, an old ceramic Tibetan teapot, and a wedding pitcher used in Brahmin weddings. On a shelf is a primitively carved wooden bird that she bought while in search of textiles: Barbara recalls how the Director of the Bolshoi fell in love with the balletic bird, and she felt guilty not to have given it to him.

The ballroom is often called 'the blue room' because of its variety of blue upholstery, blue and gold carpets, and Chinese Ming dynasty hangings. Here, too, she displays Tibetan ritual objects. Barbara is, above all, renowned in Nepal as a journalist who champions peace and unity. Her largely unknown collection attests to her artist's eye for hand-crafted beauty from diverse cultures and ethnic groups throughout Asia.

BABAR MAHAL REVISITED

Designed by architects Erich Theophile and Rohit Ranjitkar with their client Gautam SJB Rana, Babar Mahal Revisited is a re-creation of a Rana palace. Both sophisticated and welcoming, the complex has become Kathmandu's most upscale commercial venue. Original buildings that once held carriages and cows now house boutiques and galleries. New structures added to the original space borrow architectural details from a range of Rana-style buildings. Plasterwork was executed by the descendants of the same craftsmen who had plastered the original Rana palaces.

Shops and restaurants open onto intimate courtyards that hold a statue of Hanuman, a *chautara*, or a finely carved stone chaitya. Some of Kathmandu's best design is represented here at Pipalbot, Paper Moon, Tamrakar (traditional brassware), and Himalayan Textiles (showcasing Pasang Tsering's textile art). Among restaurants with cuisines that range from Latin to Japanese, the Baithak restaurant stands out as the only Nepali restaurant featuring the finest royal Rana-era recipes. A favourite dining venue in this pleasant, peaceful complex is a French-style bistro named Chez Caroline.

A statue of Hanuman greets visitors along their entry into the complex.

Brick walkways link the renovated former stables and carriage house with the newly created buildings.

ABOVE:

Here shops face outward to a courtyard with a stone chaitya carved by Jaya Raj Bajracharya and a wooden pati for visitors to take a rest.

RIGHT:

The new arched entry recreates the grandeur of the original Rana palace that had been the family home of Gautam SJB Rana. From the entry the visitor can wander at leisure through bricked lanes and courtyards to view a variety of shops, galleries, and restaurants.

THE BAITHAK RESTAURANT

OPPOSITE CLOCKWISE:

Historic photos and documents from the Rana dynasty are displayed on the bright red walls of the Baithak's reception area.

The dining room, painted a musty green, has an atmosphere of splendour belonging to an era long past.

A rakshi pitcher in a niche and historic photos decorate the reception area.

BELOW:

Niches and deep arched window wells punctuate the walls behind a lengthy dining table.

At dinner with the Rana's in the past, the table would have been set with imported silverware and glass goblets, and guests would have relished exotic dishes of wild boar, duck and even lobster, which was shipped in crates from Calcutta and portered up to Kathmandu. Today, the Baithak restaurant evokes the splendour of a by-gone era. Seated at long tables, guests savour the special Rana cuisine that had once been cooked by Brahmin female cooks called *Bajais*, and enjoy rakshi, or rice wine, poured from tall brass pitchers with slender spouts. Hung on the walls are large framed portraits of Rana rulers wearing their sophisticated formal attire and seemingly still presiding over the sumptuous banquet.

CHEZ CAROLINE

While the dishes are sophisticated, the restaurant maintains a simple open-air bistro environment. In summer large umbrellas shield guests from the sun, in winter standing heaters spread warmth even on the chilliest of evenings. Locally made tables are nestled in a brick-paved courtyard with an historic ambiance. Adapted from an image in the Garden of Dreams, a plaster Neptune with Asian eyes adorns one brick wall, while an image of the sun, from which the Ranas believed to have descended, embellishes another.

Chez Caroline's menu for the New Year features *deux tomates en tatin, chèvre et timur,* an upside-down tart of sun-dried and fresh tomatoes with imported goat cheese and timur, a unique spice that grows abundantly in the Himalayas and has medicinal properties. There is *coquilles Saint Jacques au safran et aux feuilles de curry* – roast scallops with a sauce of cream, saffron and curry leaves from a nearby tree. Also featured on the menu is *canard à l'orange revisité,* roast duck with kumquat, cardamom and orange sauce. The tart kumquats, small and perfect, are popular in Kathmandu markets in the wintertime. *Jira* (cumin seed), ginger, mint and sesame, used commonly in Nepal, feature in a number of other fusion recipes. Olive oil is produced not far from Kathmandu where a German resident has a thriving olive orchard. Arugula and other salad greens are grown in the Valley's organic farms.

Owner Caroline Sengupta gives credit for the restaurant's success to an expert Nepali team headed by Madhu the head waiter and Gopal the chef. "They have the spirit, they are the real salt of this place," says Caroline. "And Gopal is a true artist – I never create a recipe without him."

In an adapted cowshed of a former palace, Chez Caroline
serves fine food with many local organic ingredients.

THE GARDEN OF DREAMS: AN URBAN SANCTUARY

Magnificent gardens are not common to Himalayan homes. In the Kathmandu Valley clusters of dwellings were traditionally surrounded by cultivated fields, forest or grazing land. Land in cities and towns was prized – only the aristocracy could utilize valuable land for ornamental gardens. The most splendid of these has been restored after decades of neglect and decay, and opened to the public in 2006 as a tranquil oasis of peace and contemplation in the midst of Kathmandu's urban bustle.

The Garden of Dreams, also known as 'Garden of the Six Seasons' had been created in the 1920s by Field Marshal Kaiser Shumsher Rana. Passionate about horticulture and the contemporary gardens of England, he established his own within the architectural framework of six grand neo-classical pavilions, dedicated to each of the six seasons of Nepal, and embellished with ponds, fountains, trellises, urns, and statuary.

Over the years, half of the original garden has been lost to urban development. With only three of its six pavilions surviving, the remaining part was overgrown into a veritable jungle, the main pond engulfed by weeds, and many of the architectural elements crumbling. Yet in long overdue recognition of its historic significance among the great gardens of South Asia, its remaining portion finally was restored and adapted to its present purpose as a modern-day sanctuary for public recreation and edification.

The architect in charge of this transformation was Götz Hagmüller, known for his work with the Patan Museum, which exhibits his sensitivity when introducing new features and functional requirements into the given historical fabric. The architect has both restored and re-imagined Kaiser Shumsher's fantasy garden, granting it additional private spaces that free the mind and heart.

Thus, an attractive new gate takes the visitor gradually from the adjacent main road into an enclosed entrance forecourt where a simple rhomboid stone platform has been transformed into a three-tiered fountain. This also helps the acoustic transition from the traffic noise outside to the tranquil sound of falling water inside, before one obtains a full view of the garden.

In response to the existing platform and semi-circular stone steps, the architect was inspired to create an amphitheatre of stepped lawns that resemble the terraced rice paddies of Nepal.

The Basantha (spring) Pavilion seen from
the lotus pond of the Garden of Dreams.

Another innovation is the large amphitheatre created from a once
sunken garden, with grass terraces like the paddy fields of Nepal gently
stepping up from a semi-circular moat. The water supply of the central
pond was restored, and the papyrus in the four corners was supplemented
by water lilies and lotus. A lone baby plaster elephant was lifted from his
pedestal in the pond to be placed next to a plaster parent in front of the
Basantha (spring) Pavilion. A row of plaster caryatids were also given a
new life by pairing them with metal columns so that they could support
an arbor above a dining terrace. Missing her head, a plaster sphinx stands
in the centre of a pathway requesting the visitor to imagine her original
countenance and to answer the mysterious riddle, "Who am I?"

Re-emphasized in the restoration are the garden's axes: the original
symmetry is now apparent with each lengthwise and cross-wise view.
Attractive paths of stone and brick have been re-laid and new varieties of
bamboo, roses, and other cultivated plants have joined the magnificent
trees and flowering shrubs of the original garden.

The interiors of the pavilions have been re-designed to serve their
new function as restaurant space. Inside the blue interior of the Basantha

Pavilion, Hagmüller's favourite conical brass lamps hang low over the
tables. The dark-stained furniture appears to have been imported from a
Viennese café; in fact, the chairs were made locally with bent reed. The
interior of the Barkha (monsoon) Pavilion in the rear of the garden has
the high arches and vaults of a Palladian building. Its pressed tin ceiling,
which had lost its colours, was not repainted: instead, aluminum foil
serves to create a luxurious effect. A rotunda was created on a raised
platform on the garden's west end, enhancing the long view of the garden
from the Basantha Pavilion on the east end, and distracting the eye from
a far less romantic office building behind.

To the north of the garden is the palace containing the large library
of Kaiser Shumsher Rana. The interior space, with its sweeping staircase
and high ornamented ceilings, is for the most part unchanged. The high
walls display huge portraits of the elite Rana rulers as well as their
hunting trophies. The rooms belong to a lavish era that promoted a
western aesthetic that is now dated, whereas Shumsher's garden, by
comparison, has become timeless.

ABOVE:

The architect created a trellis over outdoor café tables and a brick path that leads to the garden's restaurant. Stone steps are laid over a semi-circular pond on the left.

RIGHT:

The neo-Palladian Barkha (monsoon) Pavilion, now an elegant bar. The pressed tin ceiling that had once been painted was covered with shiny aluminum foil.

OPPOSITE:

Original flowerbeds were replanted with hedge plants and pathways created with gravel. The fountain is of Hagmüller's design.

LIVING IN BHAKTAPUR

At the Brahmayani Temple one early morning during the festival of Dasain, young boys wearing loincloths, turbans, and exquisite jewellery sit motionless, balancing oil lights in a ritual of fulfilling pledges that they perform for their families. For hours, their sisters and mothers keep alit oil lamps that are attached to the boy's bodies with clumps of mud and dung. Meanwhile, grains of rice fly in the air as a crowd of worshippers make offerings to the Nava Durga deities, fierce representations of the Goddess Parvati, that are represented by the new Nava Durga masks on display in the temple. According to the anthropologist Robert Levy, Bhaktapur's manifestations of the gods can be "anchored in space or moved through it." Later in the evening, ritual dancers don the Nava Durga masks and, accompanied by musicians, move the deities through the city's small neighbourhoods.

The masks are made anew each year by a designated artist of the Chitrakar (painter) caste with special clay that is imbued with power and magic through a tantric ritual. The masks are secretly cremated each June and new ones made in September incorporate the ashes. Such notions of continuity permeate all levels of life in Bhaktapur, which has been compared to a stage where some 80 events are re-enacted each year. Following Dasain is the festival of Tihar when the city's windows glow with the light of oil lamps. Decorative pathways are drawn with chalk, mud, and powder in front of house doors, inviting Laxmi, goddess of wealth to enter. On our visit to Kuthu Math we put oil lights in all the courtyard niches and the resident caretaker offers our gold jewellery to Laxmi on a shrine we create in the TV room.

Following one of Bhaktapur's astonishing festivals, I am always happy to retreat into the calm space of a private home. The stories of two Bhaktapur homes, and the lives of their extraordinary residents, are told here. Another oasis in Bhaktapur is Kathmandu University's Department of Music where young musicians can be found practicing local instruments in a restored courtyard and garden.

KUTHU MATH

Architect Götz Hagmüller and his wife Ludmilla have made the 18th century *Kuthu Math* their home for three decades. Similar to a monastery, a *math* was a place of spiritual learning under a resident guru (*mahant*) as well as a hostel during pilgrimage time. The Hagmüllers have sensitively transformed Kuthu Math's living quarters and garden into a space for contemplation, creativity, and entertaining.

To their house we come for true rest and refuge, which is especially needed when one lives in chaotic and bustling Kathmandu. In the daytime you enjoy the peace of the garden, in the evening you may shift to relax on the roof terrace above Götz's studio with its splendid view of the snow-capped mountain range of Ganesh Himal to the north.

From this vantage point you can get a glimpse of Kuthu Math's courtyard, and also look upon one of the few remaining large tile roofs, which had dominated the roofscape of Bhaktapur until three decades ago. Quite distinct from traditional roofing techniques in other parts of the world, here the hand-made clay tiles (*djingati*) are laid in a thick layer of well-prepared mud on top of the timber roof structure, thus providing a reasonable insulation against heat and cold – an advantage that today's concrete or tin roofs certainly do not have. On the other hand, these tile-on-mud roofs are prone to fissures and leaks, and I love Kuthu Math all the more when I understand the constant effort required to maintain them.

Across the courtyard, the half-open kitchen and dining area are just barely visible under the canopy of an exuberant bougainvillea that had grown from a small sapling in a corner of the courtyard three decades ago. It turned out only later, when dowsing experts discovered the courtyard to be laid out on a geomantic and thus possibly sacred grid, that the sapling unintentionally had been planted at the exact crossing point of two of the grid's energy lines – a spot believed to be especially beneficial to plant growth and health.

We descend a ladder staircase to what was once a large dining room and rest area for pilgrims, called a *baithak*. It is now a spacious living room in which a feast of beaten rice and curries is served to Kathmandu friends on numerous Bhaktapur festival days. Unlike the elaborately carved window frames, doors and struts of Newar exteriors, their interiors are for the most part without décor. "All impulse to adorn is reserved for the outside façade," Götz explains, noting the contrasting simplicity that he is so careful to preserve.

He appreciates the intimate scale of Newar architecture: the door measurements of 130 centimetres high and 60–70 centimetres wide are almost standard in the house of a farmer, merchant, palace, or monastery. In Kuthu Math you are careful to bow your head under the door lintels.

In the room of his home once used by pilgrims (baithak), the architect took out part of the ceiling so as to create more headspace, and added windows to upper terraces, providing indirect light from above. Window seating is simply upholstered in white cotton as are floor cushions. A striking kilim laid over a series of white rugs adds colour to the room.

ABOVE:

The large baithak was used for lodging and feeding pilgrims who came to the math. Götz deliberately kept tables and seating low and informal, in keeping with traditional proportions and purpose. The double row of pillars are functional and have little decoration except for the angled section above the middle.

LEFT:

Panels of a book cabinet are covered with natural and orange-coloured Nepali paper.

OPPOSITE:

The stairway to Götz's studio is an adaptation of the traditional step ladder. Below are drawers for architectural drawings. All timber elements are stained dark, following tradition.

Yet in the baithak, Götz opened up a part of the low ceiling and brought in additional light from terraces that he created by cutting into the roofline. He has added wall niches not for practical reasons, but because "they make one appreciate the thickness of walls." At the same time, they can be used to introduce indirect lighting by holding an electric light, oil lamp or candle. Götz has created more niches in Kuthu Math than would have been traditional, especially in the kitchen which he admits was inspired by the dissolving of a thick wall into niches that he admired in vernacular Indian architecture.

Upholstery is simple white cotton, following his sense that plain natural fabrics fit best with the room's timber elements, mud floors, and walls. Furniture is low in scale, with floor seating in keeping with the customs of pilgrims. Götz claims that the Newar aesthetic matches his own, such as the age-old functional design and beauty of Newar brass and bronze objects, which he likes to collect.

When the weather is cold, dinner is served in a small dining room where lattice windows toward the courtyard provide both ventilation and privacy and can be lifted to allow two adopted cats to slip in. On the wall opposite the windows, space is virtually extended by two mirrored walls of shelves lined with reflective brass plates. Inspired by Newar brass traditions, Götz has produced brassware of his own design including handsome ladles, trays, and hanging lamps.

I tell him how I enjoy seeing the changes since my last visit. He replies that recently, he'd accomplished things he'd wanted to do for ten years – like putting in the skylight over the dining table, an idea which came to him when the roof lost some tiles and the light poured in. Noting that his house is like a laboratory, he adds, "If you are an architect, you have a particularly heavy bag on your back, thinking that you will never finish."

Hagmüller designed special wall niches with frames above for his Rajasthani paintings that are used in meditation. The niche on the left displays a traditional rakshi pitcher with cups and a tray. The niche on the right holds a Newar ritual water pitcher, oil lamp, and container for tikka powder.

An Austrian carpet beater hangs below a niche holding a brass donor statue.

A White Tara statue, lit from above, is adorned with a kata.

Above a niche holding an offering dish are paper images that were pasted on the wall during the festival of Nag Panchami to ward off evil.

THE ENCLOSED GARDEN AT KUTHU MATH

I experienced the peace of this garden when I spent a week in the Hagmüller residence during one potentially volatile national election period. The garden is hidden in the back of the residence and separated by brick walls from the neighbouring yards and buildings. Brick, stone and tile define each section of the garden, which is formed like a mandala with a circular pond in the centre. The wooden benches, brick ledges, chairs, and tables all around the garden allow the visitor to change his perch and follow the rays of the sun. Mirrors on the garden's far end create a sense of green space way beyond the limitations of the brick wall.

It is hard to imagine that once there was nothing here but level ground and crumbling old brick walls. Götz recounts the garden's beginning when he needed mud for renovation work on the house, so he dug it out of the garden. Hence a large puddle led to the notion of a central pond. And then from the central pond the garden developed in a geometrical pattern divided by raised flowerbeds and walkways. The new garden was originally meant mainly for distant appreciation and contemplation from the dining area above – only later were tables and chairs placed below and, much later, a terrace for his wife Milla to practice t'ai chi. The high back wall has translucent lattice windows, allowing even the sun's last light into the garden.

Potted plants also play a role defining space. Pots line the edge of the pond, fill wall niches, and sit on small pedestals. This is a garden that is tamed and controlled by its master, who can sit at the kitchen window above, contemplating moving a tree from here to there, changing the course of a brick path, or trimming back the bountiful azalea. The monsoon comes and does what it will, and in winter the cutting and pulling begins once more. And so continues the relationship with a great architect and his magnificent and ever-evolving private 'garden of dreams'.

The garden of Kuthu Math, tucked in amongst urban dwellings, is based on a mandala design of a square around a circle. Its geometry is delineated by tile and brick made locally. The garden's originally flat surface was modulated to create different levels. In the foreground is a platform used for the practice of t'ai chi and composed of contrasting old and new tiles.

THE GERT-MATTHIAS WEGNER HOUSE

For almost thirty years, Gert-Matthias Wegner has resided in the heart of Bhaktapur in a five-storey Newar house named *Yatachen*, meaning 'sunny place'. Like many traditional homes in the Kathmandu Valley, Yatachen has been divided between several families so that Gert now maintains four separate rent contracts for rooms that are linked by outside balconies and narrow steps. Yet his residence appears to the visitor as a whole and even encompasses a walled garden endowed with flowering plants and trees, such as camelias, that are important for Newar rituals. The walls of Yatachen are plastered with *aletsa*, a fermented mixture of cowdung, straw, and mud that keeps the house cool in summer, warm in winter. Traditional straw mats on which are displayed many of Gert's fine Tibetan and Mongolian rugs, further insulate the space.

Gert's contribution to the preservation of traditional music in Bhaktapur is known both to local residents and internationally, and he has achieved his personal dream of establishing the Kathmandu University Department of Music in Bhaktapur. He is acclaimed worldwide for his expertise in Indian and Nepal traditions of drumming. The image of this German professor leading a local band, playing the cylindrical drum of Newar farmers, the *dhimay*, will be remembered by generations of Bhaktapur Newars.

Gert is optimistic that he has at last found a tabla student to whom he will pass on the unique repertoire that was given to him by his guru during his twenty-four years' apprenticeship in Mumbai. On the morning that we visit, he and Abhaya (whose name means 'fearless') face each other in a small practice room and begin to drum. "Dhageterekete dhageterekete dhagetete GHERAN..." instructs Gert. Light enters through the windows and doorway of the low-ceilinged room, which contains a cabinet with vials of homeopathic medicine (Gert is an expert in treating maladies, such as my typical Kathmandu Valley allergy to mould). A large desk stands in the room 'for other serious work', while flanking the doorway are two magnificent tiger rugs.

The music lesson lasts an hour, and then we change venue. In the kitchen, teacher and pupil speak different dialects of Newari as Gert demonstrates how to make a South Indian lunch: Abhaya scrapes out a coconut as his teacher prepares his favourite Mysore recipe for cauliflower. He tosses a pinch of asafetida, mustard seeds, urad dal, and red and green chilies into hot oil – no need to measure. Cauliflower and a pinch of salt are added and steamed with water. The mixture is next stirred in a traditional Newar pot of heavy brass, one of a collection of pots that are very old and seldom seen anymore.

We help ourselves to seconds and thirds, relishing the chance to sit with this scholar and musician-cum-chef at his table copied locally from an English garden catalogue. The kitchen area was once the lair of local monkeys, but he has turned it into an airy space, with connecting outdoor terraces, a raised roof and large windows that flood the room with light. On the walls are carpets from Inner Mongolia and a photo of Gert's guru, Nikhil Ghosh. Later, over coffee we reflect on what a tranquil home he has created here. Yatachen, the sunny place, has provided a refuge, evolving over years of commitment and sometimes even 'intense suffering' as Gert struggled to establish his dream of a school for the study of music.

ABOVE:

Inner Mongolian carpets hang above the stairwell. Newar oil lamps stand on either side of a small Tibetan prayer table and a Tibetan carpet with lotus motifs lies in the foreground. A wall of windows allows the dining and music room to fill with light.

RIGHT:

Carved motifs on a Tibetan table in the practice room.

OPPOSITE:

Inner Mongolian and Tibetan carpets are laid on terracotta tiled floors of the dining room. A portrait of Gert's tabla guru, Nikhil Ghosh, and a Tibetan dragon pillar carpet hang above the staircase leading to the roof terrace.

CLOCKWISE:

The Dance Pavilion designed by Götz Hagmüller has the traditional shape and features of a small Newar pavilion or *mandapa*, with the roof resting on pillars around the dance platform. Structural safety against earthquakes, however, is created by a simple modern device of thin (and hardly visible) steel bars bracing the four corner pillars. The pavilion is elevated on a stone and brick platform.

A moon gate has been added at the entrance to the garden. In the temple courtyard a student plays flute nearby a stone *Nandi,* the bull that is Shiva's vehicle.

OPPOSITE:

The Newar pati in a secluded corner of the garden provides a peaceful space for music practice.

THE KATHMANDU UNIVERSITY
DEPARTMENT OF MUSIC

For hundreds of years, local music ensembles in Bhaktapur have played for Newar festivities and rituals. Today, with the number of such ensembles dwindling, the Department of Music, Kathmandu University, plays a crucial role in deepening appreciation and knowledge of Nepal's traditional music and preserving it for future generations.

In 1996 a Shiva Temple complex, built in the 19th century by a well-to-do Bhaktapur merchant, became the centre for the university's traditional music programme. Today, sixty students study classical Nepali music here and often the complex is host to various activities: players of tabla practice amongst a display of shaman drums; students from the local high school sketch the courtyard's shrines; a flautist stretches on a garden bench to play his flute; the security guard practices the shawm and the gardener digs weeds from the garden's long brick pathways – all seeming to illustrate 'points about musical instruction' that are posted on the school's bulletin board: *Induce the joy of music by way of group singing, dancing, playing musical instruments, various kinds of listening experiences and personal creation. Show how music is related to other mental and physical activities.*

The music school is comprised of separate but connected realms for study and contemplation. Intimate teaching spaces within traditional buildings have small windows opening to views of the temple courtyard and garden. The courtyard is a sacred space containing a Shiva temple, shrines of four Hindu gods, and a row of Shiva lingam concealed partly by fast-growing vegetation. A moon gate bridges the courtyard with the garden, a pavilion, and a pond. Reflected in the pond are students practicing their instruments in a traditional pati that stands in a secluded corner.

The school's 'Dance Pavilion' was designed by Götz Hagmüller and it stands in temple-like perfection amongst the pomelo trees, bamboo, and roses of the garden. Resting on a base composed of layers of rock and brick, the pavilion provides shelter for music practice on hot afternoons or during monsoon showers.

LIVING IN PATAN

Beyond the historic Patan Darbar Square, narrow streets of old Patan open on to its many courtyards or *bahals*. Bahals are a group of houses built by Newar Buddhists of the Shakya and Bajracharya castes around a temple and courtyard containing chaityas and shrines. Every morning and evening from my home in a bahal, I observe a little boy who is undergoing initiation at the Golden Temple make his rounds between a number of bahals, barefoot in even the coldest of months, ringing his hand-bell. During the annual event of *mata-ya puja* (the Festival of Lights), hundreds of Patan's male residents rush by in a procession, carrying lighted tapers and offerings as they visit and prostrate before the city's important Buddhist sites that include 600 chaityas.

Throughout the day I hear the tap-tap-tap as the craftsmen next door make exquisite Buddhist statues and ritual objects. Living in Patan one is witness to rituals and art traditions that are centuries old and still part of modern life. Uko Bahal, where small workshops are busy all the time, produces some of the world's finest metalwork. Treasures of metalcraft are found in Patan's palaces, temples, shrines, and hitis. Famous also for carvings in wood and stone Patan is often referred to as a living museum.

Newar communities in Patan work together to preserve their heritage, with some projects carried out by organizations such as the Kathmandu Valley Preservation Trust. Artisans are able to replicate elements of ancient architecture, or create statues and thangkas according to tradition. At the same time many are finding ways to innovate, as shown in the stonecarving by Jaya Raj Bajracharya and the collaboration between Patan artisans Rajan Shakya, Rubin Shakya, and designer Wendy Marston.

A traditional Newar brick building with carved wooden windows facing the Patan Darbar. The rooms on the ground floor have been converted to shops for handicrafts and a top floor was added later.

OPPOSITE TOP ROW:

Masks of the Dipankara Buddha adorned with flowers during the celebration of samyak.

OPPOSITE BOTTOM:

In the ihi ceremony, a young girl is ritually married to a bel fruit.

A Newar woman in Patan who reached 88 years, 8 months and 8 days celebrates her bura janko ceremony.

The Usnisa Vijaya mandala created for a bura janko with Navagraha (9 planets) represented in surrounding baskets.

Relatives of a woman who celebrates her first bura janko ceremony (at 77 years, 7 months and 7 days) carry her in a palanquin to see and be seen by the deities in Patan's temples.

ABOVE:

Men prepare the tower of the chariot of the Rato Machhindranath, binding tree poles together with special vines. Rato (Red) Machhindranath is the god of rain, beloved by the Kathmandu Valley's Newars.

RIGHT:

The wooden-wheeled Rato Macchindranath chariot, with its 60-foot tower, creates excitement and drama as it is pulled through the crowded streets of Patan.

PATAN'S RITUALS AND FESTIVALS

Living in a Patan bahal, I often see my neighbours bearing trays of grains, coins, fruits, flowers and powders as they take part in rituals that mark stages in the cycle of life. One day, five-year old Nani appears dressed as a bride in red and gold silk cloth: she is to be married to a *bel* fruit in the *ihi* ceremony that unites her with a divine groom and the soul of her future husband. Later that month, her grandmother, having reached 77 years, 7 months and 7 days, climbs into a decorated palanquin to be paraded through the bahals. She is having her *bura janko* ceremony. The gods are now bringing new energy to this phase of my elderly neighbour's life, and for the first time since being a widow she can wear red tikka powder and gold jewellery.

The magnificent *samyak* festival takes place every four years. Dozens of Dipankara Buddha images are carried in procession from bahal to bahal, some supported by men who climb into their wooden framed bodies and silk robes. Later the Buddhas gather in our courtyard where people come to greet them as if they were important guests, dabbing tikka powder on their gilt copper faces and setting flowers in their crowns.

In early spring there is the biggest event in Patan, the journey of the chariot of Rato Macchindranath, an immense wooden wheeled chariot and tower that is pulled through the city's narrow streets. Inevitably it creates traffic jams and brings down vital electric wires, but the slow progress of the ancient wheels transporting a precariously leaning tower and a sacred shrine captivates our attention for weeks.

LIVING ARTS OF PATAN

Patan's Uku Bahal exhibits some of the city's finest works in metal and wood. Dating from the 6th century, it is one of the oldest bahals, with statues and other components of the monastery complex added over time. The main shrine of Uku Bahal contains a metal image of Aksobhya, one of the five wisdom buddhas, with a red face and covered with ornaments. A smaller Aksobhya sits below. The repoussé door dates from the 17th century. Typically above a shrine door is a torana (tympanum) that bears images of deities as well as snakes and *makaras* (mythological water creatures).

Bishwo Rathur, pictured here in his small workshop making wax models for casting, is one of the Patan artisans who continues the statue-making traditions in Patan.

AT WORK WITH PATAN'S MASTERS

Artist and animal lover Wendy Marston came to Nepal over thirty years ago with her husband, British Army Major Robin Marston. Theirs is a home of unique surprises: around the coffee table two ducks pursue an anxious chicken; on a counter in the kitchen an ancient goat is munching dinner; in the garden the donkey recently rescued from a brick factory has just given birth. But such scenes no longer faze the artisans who come and go from their workshops in Patan and Bhaktapur: they bear gilded lizards to ornament jewellery boxes covered in green lizard skin, ostrich eggs painted with Tibetan clouds, gold and pearl necklaces replicating those of past Nepalese queens, silver walnuts, figs and mangosteens, and the most splendid of Himalayan-inspired bowls, plates and serving utensils.

Wendy works closely with Newar woodcarvers, jewellers, painters, carpenters, and metal artists (wax casters, carvers, gilders and specialists in repoussé) to produce innovative crafts of the highest quality. She routinely meets to check progress and to share her latest inspiration with Prem, Raju, Rubin, Ramesh, Ranjit, Santosh, Radeysham, and other expert craftspeople she has known for many years. Her invention is proven in the details – the brass dorje used as a cabinet handle, or the use of traditionally etched bamboo poles for the handles of serving spoons.

CLOCKWISE:

Wendy's cabinets combine fine painting by Raju Shakya and metalwork by Rubin Shakya. Here painted hands hold brass dorjes that are the cabinet handles.

In the garden of the Marston home, Ganesh's vehicle, the shrew, holds a *laddu*, the favourite sweet of the elephant god. This replica of a shrew in the Patan Museum was produced by Rubin Shakya.

Raised gesso work and a 24-carat fire-gilded earring give dimension to a cabinet depicting Goddess Tara. The cabinet combines the fine craftsmanship of a carpenter, metalworker, and painter.

CLOCKWISE:

A ladle with a fire-etched bamboo handle made by Dalits, people of untouchable castes from the Nepal hills, complements brass and silver Tibetan-style serving bowls and dishes.

Bowls of reconstituted amber are embellished with repoussé work in pure silver. The spoon is modelled after a holy water spoon carried by Buddhist monks.

This plate's intricate pattern is created with one piece of silver using an old cut-out technique. The rim is fire-gilded with 24-carat gold.

Hammered silver salad servers have etched bamboo handles.

A silver rice-serving spoon is influenced by a Persian design. Traditional Tibetan wooden tea cups inspire the style of a wooden bowl with a silver interior.

RUBIN SHAKYA
LOST-WAX CASTING MASTER

ABOVE:

A seated monkey holding a jackfruit at Uku Bahal Monastery, Patan. The image relates to a story in the Jataka Tales, Buddhist stories with ethical teachings. A collection of statues by Wendy Marston and Rubin Shakya includes a reproduction of this popular statue, which is found in several temples in Patan.

Rubin Shakya discusses a lost-wax cast statue with Wendy at his workshop in Patan.

PREM BAHADUR NAGARKOTHI
MASTER SILVERSMITH

LEFT:

Prem Bahadur Nagarkothi created this intricate pattern in 100 per cent silver on the bottom of a Tibetan-style wooden bowl. The silverwork is all made from one piece and the pattern is based on a traditional design that Wendy and Prem revived. Bottoms of bowls or cups are traditionally finely decorated because they are displayed upside down.

RAJU SHAKYA
MASTER PAINTER

CLOCKWISE:

Raju Shakya is a thangka painter who extends his skills to painting furniture. Here he paints a cabinet designed by Wendy Marston depicting the Arhats, the original disciples of Buddha.

Handles of this cabinet's doors are fashioned like cymbals, which are held by monks who accompany the great Tibetan Buddhist practitioner and poet Milarepa.

The raised gesso technique is used on jewellery, ornaments and other details of a painted cabinet to give dimension and texture. Here, Raju has depicted *yab-yum*, the male deity and his female consort who symbolize the union of wisdom and compassion.

The brass handle on a cabinet depicting the Arhats is made by Rubin Shakya and represents a lotus.

A PATAN FAMILY STONE CARVING TRADITION

Patan is world-renowned for its Newar artists and craftspeople. Stone carvers, wood carvers, metal casters, and jewellery makers – all are found in tiny rooms in their bahals working just as their ancestors did for centuries. Especially thriving is Patan's tradition of metalwork: many of the lost-wax cast images found in the monasteries across the Himalayas and today in those of Europe originated in Patan. Uku Bahal, whose centre of spiritual life is the Newar Buddhist temple Rudra Varna Mahavir, is home to some of the most famous Newar sculpting and casting families.

Patan stonecarving master, Jaya Raj Bajracharya, is pictured above on the left with his father, wife and daughter who are also stone carvers. His grandfather, Buddha Raj, carved some of the beautiful votive chaityas at the temple of Swayambhunath. Jaya Raj continues to make chaityas for people who wish to commemorate their dead. He also created two chaityas for Kathmandu's Hyatt hotel that was built in the vicinity of Bouddhanath stupa. Niels Gutschow, architect and author of *The Nepalese Caitya*, together with Nepalese master stone carvers, designed this unique installation.

ABOVE:

The Patan stone-carving family of Jaya Raj Bajracharya stands amongst votive chaityas at Swayambhunath that were carved by his grandfather. Pictured from left are Jaya Raj, his father Lok Raj, daughter Jenisha, and wife Sarmila.

OPPOSITE:

Jaya Raj was commissioned to carve some of the stupas in an interior courtyard of Bouddhanath's Hyatt hotel.

THE KATHMANDU VALLEY PRESERVATION TRUST

The Kathmandu Valley Preservation Trust works to preserve the Patan Darbar's Royal Palace Complex, as well as other great treasures of Kathmandu Valley art and architecture. On their computers in an old Rana building facing the Patan Darbar, a number of KVPT's technical staff will be found hard at work making drawings and plans, while others are busy on site in the Darbar Palace Complex.

KVPT's office rooms retain their original Rana-era details. The library and meeting room was once used for piano recitals. The plaster depictions of angels over the room's arches were once brightly coloured, but are now painted over with a thin coat of white paint. Stencil patterns decorate the ceiling beams. Wall niches have been adapted for display of books and periodicals.

A NEWAR HOME IN PATAN

Architect Rohit Ranjitkar, KVPT's programme director, lives near the KVPT office in a multi-storey residential building, which he has renovated and enhanced through the addition of more traditional elements: a wood stove, wall niches, carved wooden columns, and doors. Thick mud floors have been replaced with planks of reclaimed wood, thus increasing room height. Old wood was also used to build furniture such as a dining room table whose legs are made from old columns and brackets. As they would have been in the past, furnishings are low and simple. Utilizing historical design elements, the house feels traditionally hand-crafted and at the same time contemporary.

CLOCKWISE:

Wooden columns, niches, and a ladder staircase were added by Rohit when he created an open dining and living space. Double columns are a typical feature of the traditional baithak, a large room for dining and resting.

The traditional staircase with brass railing leads to bedrooms on the floor above.

A display of brass door knobs produced in a workshop on the ground floor of Rohit's home.

ABOVE:

A living and guest room is decorated with black and white historical photos of Valley architecture and Rohit's collection of antique brass oil lamps. The wooden floor is covered with hand-woven straw mats (sukul).

RIGHT:

Lit niches hold traditional Newar brass pitchers. The legs of the dining table and benches are made with old wooden columns.

ABOVE:

The view over Patan Darbar from Erich's terrace.

LEFT:

A small sitting area is two steps higher than the bedroom. Sliding glass doors open to the terrace and simple white curtains on dowels filter light and create privacy.

OPPOSITE:

Cushions and a blanket from Himachal Pradesh allow for casual seating on Nepali straw mats. Walls, ceiling, and curtains are white, pleasantly lightening the space and contrasting with the dark hard wood used for doors, floors, and windows.

Above the offices of the Kathmandu Valley Preservation Trust, with a view over Patan Darbar Square, is the apartment of Erich Theophile, the founder of the KVPT and of H. Theophile, a high-end hardware company that originated in Nepal. Erich, who now spends most of his time in New York City, has created a comfortable living space with one of the world's greatest views. Traditional mats (sukul) cover the floor, topped by a long woolen blanket from Himachal Pradesh. Colours in Erich's apartment are light and subdued, except for the deep hues of Asian textiles.

Yogurt, purchased from the market in unfired ceramic bowls, is served on the terrace at breakfast, while the menu for lunch ranges from *roti* and curry to wood-fired pizzas with arugula and goat cheese. Guests are also entertained indoors in a cozy sitting area on a raised platform next to the terrace. Furniture is low, with benches softened by cushions. In the evening, candles are lit on Erich's tall candleholders that are modelled after Newar oil lamps, and outside the terrace's glass doors the streetlights on the Patan Darbar allow for a spectacular view of tiered temple roofs.

COLOURFUL LIVING IN A PATAN BAHAL

North of the Patan Darbar Square, in a traditional Newar bahal, KVPT Co-Executive Director Thomas Schrom revamped a six-storey house to create a living space with a view of the Himalayas and most of the city. His renovation reflects his love and knowledge of building and carpentry. The bright orange kitchen on the fourth floor is the heart of the home and is reached by an old wood staircase. Thomas has extended the kitchen space in every way possible. He replaced a cement wall with glass doors so that the kitchen opens out to a terrace. The long dining table made of two wide planks is set on rollers so that it can be partly pushed back over the stairwell when not in use for entertaining. A shelf built out over the stairwell allows for extra storage space, and wall niches were chiselled to make room for the refrigerator and water dispenser. Visitors are entertained with meals that include ingredients such as galanghal and kaffir lime from Bangkok, Kashmiri chili and fish masala from Goa, and tea leaf salad from Burma. Tableware is made in Thimi, a Newar town near Bhaktapur.

Below the kitchen is a guest bedroom whose mud floor is covered with striped blankets produced in Nepal's remote district of Dolpo. A carved wooden chest brought down by porters from Humla District stands at one end of the room, beneath a tussar silk sari from Orissa that is used as a wall-hanging. The room contains the treasures gathered on treks and other journeys around Asia: shaligrams (the holy ammonites found within round stones in the Himalayas), Tibetan boxes, shamans' hats, textiles from Gujarat, and Bhutanese bamboo boxes. Throughout the home colours – strong shades of orange, yellow, red and blue – are used freely. In the midst of the constant activity of the bahal, the dwelling provides a sense of a world both connected and apart, and an exuberant amalgamation of East and West.

OPPOSITE:

Glass doors of the kitchen open to a terrace. Counter tops and floors are polished with red wax and walls are painted brightly.

RIGHT:

Brass vessels from Nepal and Tibetan spice boxes line a kitchen shelf.

BELOW:

In the bedroom, blankets from Dolpo cover an old mud floor. A wooden statue of Hanuman sits on a carved wooden chest from Humla. The wall hanging is a sari from Orissa. A reproduction of a drawing of a chaitya in Patan by Robert Powell hangs in a stairwell outside the room's painted red doors.

A PATAN TABLE

ABOVE: Thomas Schrom's kitchen uses a variety of utensils and containers hand-made in the Himalayas. Ceramic plates are by Thimi Ceramics, designed by Ani Kasten. The kitchen opens onto a terrace and a Tibetan chest is used as a buffet table.

BOTTOM ROW FROM LEFT: Brass ladles and spoons designed by Götz Hagmüller; local ingredients used for cooking include flowers from the Koiralo tree *(Bauhinia variegata)*; a brass vessel on a runner of dhaka cloth, both made in Nepal; Indian and Burmese pots for salt and spices; Tibetan and Bhutanese butter containers.

ACKNOWLEDGMENTS

We thank all the people represented in our book who welcomed us into their homes and workplaces and shared with us their experiences living in the Himalayas. A generous Himalayan community spirit was extended to us wherever we photographed.

A special thanks goes to Götz Hagmüller for his inspiration and guidance throughout this project, and to Meryl Dowman, Pam Ross, Kabir Mansingh Heimsath, Nancy Ekholm Burkert, Rand Burkert, and Janet Bush for their advice and careful reading and editing of the text.

My husband Thomas Schrom helped to conceptualize this project, provided us with steady support throughout the making of the book, patiently answered hundreds of my questions, and finalized all elements of the book design. Nikki and Priti Thapa were invaluable members of our team – we could not have realized this book without their skills in photo-editing, organization, and overall dedication. John Harrison used his vast Himalayan knowledge to draw us a map and to inform us about architecture in Ladakh.

John Hubbard designed a beautiful layout and advised us on final production, and our agent Barbara Cox gave us steady support throughout the process of making and publishing this book.

Rinchen Dorje and Tshering Wangchuk Maurer assisted our explorations of Bhutan, and the staff of the Amankora kindly welcomed us to photograph the Amankora lodges. Monisha Ahmed, Wangchuk Fargo, Amchi Tsewang Wangchuk, Gerald Kozicz, André Alexander, and Gurmit Tsewang contributed greatly to the success of our remarkable journey in Ladakh. Chris Buckley, Uttara Sarkar Crees, Kun Kun Duan, Ed Jocelyn, Hwang Eu-fung, and Jeff Fuchs supported our research on Tibetan culture in the TAR and Gyalthang. Bijoy Jain and Vatsal Vakaria of Studio Mumbai, and Shakti Himalaya generously shared with us their experience creating 360 Leti. Jaya Raj Bajracharya, Ellen Coon, Luca and Camilla Corona, Carroll Dunham, Ian Alsop, Charles Gay, Christopher Giercke, James Giambrone, Niels Gutschow, Frances Howland, Tim Linkins, Wendy Marston, Rohit Ranjitkar, John Sanday, Caroline Sengupta, Mary Slusser, Dev Tamrakar, Erich Theophile, Sangeeta Thapa, Pia and Karma Tashi, and Gert-Matthias Wegner are among the dear friends in Nepal who shared with us their wealth of knowledge of Himalayan art, culture, and religion.

This book is dedicated to Robert and Nancy Burkert, whose wisdom, encouragement and love gave impetus and constant support to this project, and to Carroll, Liam, and Galen.

In Chhunggar village, bold vertical stripes of the three protectors are painted on a chorten and across the rocks at its base.

The time-worn face of a well-known
monkey statue at Uku Bahal Temple
in Patan, Nepal.

aletsa – the Newari name for plaster made of cow dung, straw, and mud

allo – wild nettle, used to make textiles

arga – a clay used in Tibet to waterproof rooftops

bahal – a monastery courtyard containing shrines and chaityas and surrounded by houses of Buddhist Newars of the priest castes

baithak – a large room used for lodging and feeding pilgrims

boo (bogh) and ka – decorative features of Bhutanese architecture. Boo are square end beams painted with mantras and ka are the spaces in between, usually painted with a floral motif.

chaitya or caitya – an architectural Buddhist monument signifying Buddhist doctrine

chang – a beer made with a grain such as millet

chautara – a resting place under the shade of two trees, the pipul and barra, who represent the female and male principle

choesham – an altar in Bhutan

chorten – Tibetan word for chaitya

chuba – a traditional Tibetan robe or dress

dhal bhat – lentils and rice, a staple of Nepal and common to the Himalayan region

dhimay – a cylindrical drum played by Newars of Nepal

dido – millet paste, typical of Sherpa cuisine

dung chen – long trumpets used by monks in Tibetan Buddhist ceremonies

dorje – an object used in Tibetan rituals representing the thunderbolt

dzong – a fortified building in Bhutan that has both secular and religious functions

ekra – a term used in Bhutan for the wattle and daub construction that is a common feature of Bhutanese architecture

gajura – a pinnacle on temple roofs, shaped like a stupa

garra – the handle for a butter churn in Nepal, usually finely carved

ga'u – an amulet, often bejewelled, and worn as a necklace by Buddhist women of the Himalayas

gho – the official traditional dress worn by Bhutanese men

gyeltsen – a victory banner that is a spire on temple buildings

harmika – the square section on top of the dome of a stupa, on which the eyes of Buddha may be painted

hiti – a stepwell, the community water source in the Kathmandu Valley

kachhen – tapering columns in Bhutanese and Tibetan temple architecture

kata – a ceremonial scarf used in Buddhist rituals

khar – an early fortress in Tibet

kholi – a central doorway with a frame carved with images of Hindu gods typical of northern Indian architecture

kira – women's traditional dress in Bhutan, consisting of a wrapped multi-panelled woven cloth, pinned at the shoulder and belted

kora – circumambulation path around a monastery complex or stupa

lhakhang – temple or shrine

linga, lingam – wood or stone shaft, symbol of Shiva, signifying creative power and the transmutation of sexual energy into spiritual energy

lokta – Nepali name for the daphne plant that is used for paper making

losar – the Tibetan New Year

lubang – house for the lu, a spirit residing in the earth an protecting the water sources

lung-ta – wind horse

mandapa – pavilion

mahant – the priest who resides in a math

makara – mythological water creature, frequently depicted in Newar water architecture and on tympanums in the Kathmandu Valley

mani stone – stone carved with a sacred mantra, placed along pilgrimage routes on walls and around chortens

math – a Hindu Newar priest's house in Nepal

melong – a metal disk symbolizing a mirror

momo – a steamed dumpling

mudra – a symbolic hand gesture of Hindu and Buddhist deities

naga – a serpent or snake

nambu – Tibetan cloth made of sheep's wool

nandi – the bull, Lord Shiva's vehicle

nay dom – a bed with painted wooden sides used in aristocratic homes

pataal – slate roofs sealed with mud, typical of Kumaoni houses

pangden – striped woolen apron worn over the chuba by Tibetan women

pantangans – stone paved courtyards of houses in the Kumaon region

pati – a traditional rest house for pilgrims and travellers in Nepal

penbey – the red frieze or band, often comprised of tamarisk twigs, a feature of Tibetan-style religious or important buildings. In Bhutan this feature is called a kemar band

puri – an Indian deep fried bread

rabsel – a projecting window balcony, a common architectural feature of Bhutanese buildings

rakshi – Nepali rice wine

sukul – a straw mat used as floor covering in Nepal

thukpa – Tibetan noodle soup

tigma – a cross motif stamped on cloth in Tibet

tikka – a mark on the forehead made in coloured powder by Hindus and Buddhists

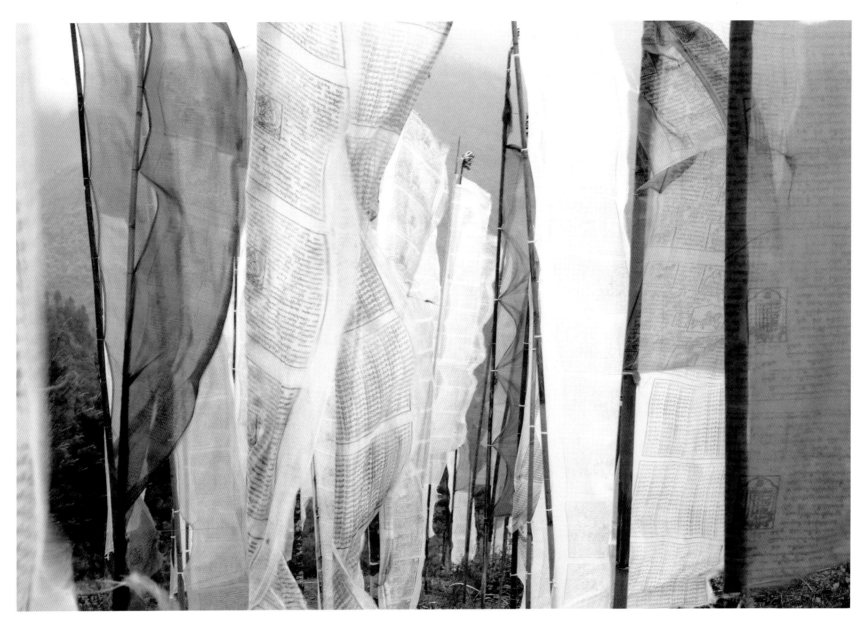

ABOVE:

Prayer flags on bamboo poles on a ridge above Trongsa, Bhutan.

LEFT:

At Ringa Monastery, Yunnan Province, wooden printing blocks and natural clay are used to print prayer flags.

SELECTED BIBLIOGRAPHY

Alexander, André. 2005. *The Temples of Lhasa: Tibetan Buddhist Architecture from the 7th to the 21st Centuries*. London: Serindia Publications.

Ahmed, Monisha and Clare Harris (ed). 2005. *Ladakh: Culture at the Crossroads*. Mumbai: Marg Publications.

Architectural Heritage Journal: 1, 2006. Division for Conservation and Cultural Heritage, Department of Culture, Ministry of Home and Cultural Affairs, Royal Government of Bhutan.

Amundsen, Ingun Bruskeland. 2003. *On Sacred Architecture and the Dzongs of Bhutan: Tradition and Transition in the Architectural History of the Himalayas*. Oslo: Oslo School of Architecture.

Beer, Robert. 1999. *The Encyclopedia of Tibetan Symbols and Motifs*. London: Serindia Publications.

Buckley, Chris. 2005. *Tibetan Furniture*. London: Thames and Hudson.

Choden, Kunzang and Walter Roder. 2006. *The Ogyen Choling Museum*. Thimpu: The Ogyen Choling Museum.

Cummings, Joe. 2001. *Buddhist Stupas in Asia: The Shape of Perfection*. Victoria: Lonely Planet Publications.

Dowman, Keith. 1995. *Power Places of Kathmandu: Hindu and Buddhist Holy Sites in the Sacred Valley of Nepal*. London: Thames and Hudson.

Dunham, Carroll. 1987. *The Hidden Himalayas*. New York: Abbeville Press.

Gutschow, Niels, Bernard Kolver, Ishwaranand Shresthacarya. 1987. *Newar Towns and Buildings*. St. Augustin: VGH Wissenshaftverlag.

Gutschow, Niels. 2011. *Architecture of the Newars: A History of Building Typologies and Details in Nepal*. Chicago: Serindia Publications.

Hagmüller, Götz. 2002. *Patan Museum: The Transformation of a Royal Palace in Nepal*. London: Serindia Publications.

Harrison, John. 1996. *Himalayan Buildings Recording Vernacular Architecture*. Kathmandu: British Council and Goethe Institute.

Kamansky, David, ed. 2004. *Wooden Wonders: Tibetan Furniture in Secular and Religious Life*. Pasedena: Pacific Asian Museum.

Korn, Wolfgang. 1976. *The Traditional Architecture of the Kathmandu Valley*. Kathmandu: Ratna Pustak Bhandar.

Larson, Knud and Amund Sinding-Larsen. 2001. *The Lhasa Atlas: Traditional Tibetan Architecture and Townscape*. London: Serindia Publications.

Levy, Robert I., with the collaboration of Kedar Raj Rajopadhyaya. 1992. *Mesocosm: Hinduism and the Organization of a Traditional Newar City in Nepal*. Delhi: Motilal Banarsidass Publishers Pvt. Ltd.

Matthiessen, Peter and Thomas Laird. 1995. *East of Lo Monthang: In the Land of Mustang*. Hong Kong: Timeless Books.

Oppitz, Mark, ed. 2001. *Robert Powell: Himalayan Drawings*. Zurich: Volkerkundemuseum Zurich.

Rael, Ronald. 2009. *Earth Architecture*. New York: Princeton University Press.

Rana, Gautam SJB, Pashupati SJB Rana, Prabhakar SJB Rana. 2003. *The Ranas of Nepal*. New Delhi: Timeless Books.

Schicklgruber, Christian. 2009. *The Tower of Trongsa: Religion and Power in Bhutan*. Ghent: Snoeck Publishers.

Schicklgruber, Christian and Françoise Pommaret, eds. 1997. *Bhutan: Mountain Fortress of the Gods*. New Delhi: Bookwise (India) Pvt. Ltd.

Slusser, Mary Shepherd. 1982. *Nepal Mandala: A Cultural Study of the Kathmandu Valley*. Princeton: Princeton University Press.

Slusser, Mary Shepherd. 2010. *The Antiquity of Nepalese Wood Carving: A Reassessment*. Seattle: University of Washington Press.

Toffin, Gerard, ed. 1991. *Man and his House in the Himalayas*. New Delhi: Sterling Publishers Pvt. Ltd.

Vitali, Robert. 1999. *Earth Door Sky Door: Paintings of Mustang by Robert Powell*. London: Serindia Publications.